THE UNPLUGGED FAMILY ACTIVITY BOOK

60+ SIMPLE CRAFTS & RECIPES FOR YEAR-ROUND FUN

RACHEL JEPSON WOLF

FAIR WINDS

DEDICATION

To the inspiring families of the Milwaukee Coalition for Children's Mental Health. May your futures shine as brightly as your hearts. In memory of Alan Slavick, whose unplugged life—lived with passion, joy, and an unflagging sense of adventure—inspires us daily.

Inspiring | Educating | Creating | Entertaining

Brimming with creative inspiration, how-to projects, and useful information to enrich your everyday life, Quarto Knows is a favorite destination for those pursuing their interests and passions. Visit our site and dig deeper with our books into your area of interest: Quarto Creates, Quarto Cooks, Quarto Homes, Quarto Lives, Quarto Drives, Quarto Explores, Quarto Gifts, or Quarto Kids.

© 2020 Quarto Publishing Group USA Inc.
Text and Photography © 2020 Rachel Jepson Wolf

First Published in 2020 by Fair Winds Press, an imprint of The Quarto Group, 100 Cummings Center, Suite 265-D, Beverly, MA 01915, USA.
T (978) 282-9590 F (978) 283-2742 QuartoKnows.com

Fair Winds Press titles are also available at discount for retail, wholesale, promotional, and bulk purchase. For details, contact the Special Sales Manager by email at specialsales@quarto.com or by mail at The Quarto Group, Attn: Special Sales Manager, 100 Cummings Center, Suite 265-D, Beverly, MA 01915, USA.

24 23 22 21 20   1 2 3 4 5

ISBN: 978-1-59233-943-3

Digital edition published in 2020
eISBN: 978-1-63159-867-8

Library of Congress Cataloging-in-Publication Data is available.

Design and Page Layout: Laura Klynstra
Photography: Rachel Jepson Wolf
Illustration: Lucky Nielson

Printed in China

CONTENTS

INTRODUCTION

THERE'S A WHOLE WORLD OUT THERE

Whether you're discovering new recipes, turning in schoolwork, playing video games, or learning a foreign language, the digital world is a part of modern life. Our cell phones, tablets, and computers are marvels at keeping the information (and, often, fun) flowing in our lives.

At the same time, the *natural world* is an integral part of our everyday life. It's just one that we, sometimes, forget to notice. Nature is there, humming along in the background as we go about our days—waiting, perhaps, for us to tune in and take note. From the busiest of cities to the tranquil, quiet countryside, nature is there. It serves as the unwavering backdrop to our daily lives.

Although we often consider nature as something existing separate from us, humans are a part of nature. Nature is where we come from, and it was our first home. By reconnecting ourselves with the Earth, sky, and seasons, we can remember our place in the natural world.

STRESS LESS

When we make time to connect with nature, both children and adults feel a greater sense of peace and a reduction in stress. Out in nature, we can hear our own quiet thoughts, get in touch with our creativity, and connect more deeply with family and friends. To rediscover nature, however, we need to put away other distractions and reacquaint ourselves with the physical world.

Even the simple act of expressing our creativity can be healing. Like nature, the creative process—activities like drawing, painting, or crafting—are known to reduce stress and anxiety. That's something that can benefit us at any age.

OFFLINE MAGIC

Unplugging (putting away our digital distractions) helps us reconnect with nature and be present in our physical realm. Without the distraction of screens, we can dive deep into the joy we experience when our heads, hearts, and hands are engaged with the world around us. Spending time without technology can also help us connect with our family and friends and feed our imaginations and curiosity as we savor the simple pleasures of screen-free play.

"But wait," you say. "Can't we do all of these things *online* as well?" Of course we can! Technology is a wonderful tool for connecting with loved ones near and far and for fueling our curiosity, imagination, and knowledge. But there is a balance to be found in this modern world by inviting in a bit of the slowness that exists in life beyond the screen. Not by doing away with technology, but by cultivating balance in our day-to-day lives.

LET'S BEGIN

If you're already living an unplugged lifestyle, if your screen time is minimal, or if you're simply a natural at unplugged play, you're ready to dive in to the chapters that follow. Grab your kitchen or craft supplies and get started with a recipe, activity, or seasonal celebration.

But, if screens are your go-to when you're looking for fun, read on for a few tips to help you get off and running with unplugged play— no batteries required!

POWER-DOWN AND POWER-THROUGH

If you're accustomed to having easy access to the internet, it might be tricky to make the leap into unplugged fun. If so, take the Power-Down and Power-Through Challenge! To play, turn off your computer, phone, or tablet, or give it to a grown-up for safekeeping (invite them to join you by powering down their device as well!).

Set a timer, challenging yourself to go screen free for a set time. Start with 30 minutes, 1 hour, or the whole afternoon. How long can you go without reaching for your device? Set a new goal each day, working your way up to longer and longer stretches of unplugged play.

Can you power through the discomfort of screen-free time and find delight in the offline world? If not, be patient with yourself. Change can sometimes be hard, and learning a new way to play might take some warming up to.

While your device is powered off, pay attention to what you're most inspired to do (aside from switching it back on, that is). What offline activities speak to you? Art, sports, books, nature, music, or conversation . . . there are countless enjoyable options of ways to spend your time.

Go outside, do a project in this book, or play a board game with a friend. Keep your head and hands occupied while you're offline, and before you know it, you'll be engrossed in a new activity and the time will fly.

UNPLUGGED PLAY

Each chapter of this book is brimming with simple, accessible ideas for engaging, offline fun. Some activities can be done alone, while others are more fun with another member of your family or a friend. But it doesn't end there! Here are a dozen of my family's favorite unplugged activities that don't require any instructions at all. What would you add to the list?

1. Take a walk or a bike ride.
2. Read a book.
3. Make art (draw, paint, sculpt, etc.).
4. Explore a nearby park or natural area.
5. Play an outdoor game (tag, Frisbee, catch, etc.).
6. Cook or bake a treat.
7. Make or listen to music, or have a dance party.
8. Play cards, puzzles, charades, or a board game.
9. Take turns telling stories.
10. Write and mail a letter.
11. Build a blanket fort (indoors or out).
12. Play with a pet.

SEASONAL RHYTHMS

As we begin to reconnect with the physical and natural world, most of us will start to notice the subtle shifts that occur within us along with the changing of the seasons. In winter, we may be drawn toward warm and cozy comfort foods, or long days reading books beneath a pile of blankets. Summer weather, on the other hand, might draw us outside to lounge in the sunshine or wriggle our toes in the warm sand or cool grass. Does spring call you outside to plant seeds or play in puddles? Does autumn beg for raking leaf piles and lighting a campfire? Listen to your seasonal rhythm to find out what each time of year evokes in you.

CELEBRATING THE SEASONS

People throughout the world have lived by the seasons for thousands and thousands of years. Meaningful historic celebrations were timed to mark the turning of the year, many of which are still celebrated today. Planting and harvesting times, the longest night, and the peak of high summer—all these and more were a cause for celebration by our ancestors on every continent and continue to be today. Why not join in the fun? Each chapter includes plans for a seasonal celebration to share with family or friends.

FOR PARENTS AND CAREGIVERS

Unplugged family time can be fun, rewarding, and memorable. Playing together outside, cooking as a family, creating simple crafts, and celebrating the seasons are the moments that your family will cherish and remember.

Rediscovering low-tech fun can be challenging for adults and kids alike! If your family is used to unrestricted screen time, give yourself and the kids in your life space to find the fun at your own pace.

Need a little guidance? Perhaps the information that follows can smooth some of the bumps along your journey toward simple, unplugged family fun.

HOW TO? IT'S UP TO YOU!

So, you're ready to help your family unplug and take a deep dive into creativity, seasonal exploration, and rediscovering the pleasures of life offline. Hooray! The next question to be answered, of course, is how to go about it.

The way you or your child press "pause" on screen time is totally up to you. There's no magic formula for the one right way to do it, and in the end, you need to find a method that works for *your* family. Some people find that small, gradual changes are easiest, while others find a more dramatic, quick shift is the simplest method for achieving change.

Whatever your approach, here are a few ideas that my family and friends have found helpful on their own journeys toward a little less screen time and a whole lot more connection.

CHECK YOUR DEVICE AT THE DOOR

Place a basket in the entryway of your house. When anyone (adult or child) enters, they drop their device in the basket. This simple shift can cause a huge change in the culture of your home, with people reaching out to one another more and reaching out for their devices less.

LOW-TECH MEALTIME

If devices are used regularly in your home, carve out a sacred screen-free zone in your kitchen during dinnertime. Set regular mealtimes and then power off all devices before sitting down to eat. Reminiscent of my mom unplugging the telephone during our dinners in the 1980s, it delivers the message "family comes first" and is a simple way to return to the ritual of the uninterrupted family meal.

UNPLUGGED PLAY DAY

Schedule a regular unplugged day to spend together as a family. Choose a weekly, monthly, or seasonal rhythm and then work together to plan fun outings, games, and meals throughout the day. With practice and planning, it will become a day you all look forward to.

MEDIA ALLOWANCE

Consider a daily or weekly media ration for a child who is struggling with limiting screen time. When my kids were younger, they each received a few wooden tokens with a time allotment written on each. They would save up their "allowance" to cash in media time later in the week. Not only did it limit the amount of time they spent online, but they practiced both saving skills and delayed gratification by rationing their allotment. How much time you give your child, of course, is completely up to you.

GAME NIGHT

One evening each week my family makes homemade pizza for dinner. We take turns choosing a favorite card game or board game and then spend the meal nibbling pizza as we laugh and play together. The pizza toppings and game selections may be different each week, but one thing that never changes is that it's everyone's favorite, fun, family dinner.

MODERATION MATTERS

Is *zero media* the answer to a happy family and harmonious home? I don't think so. My own mom taught me to honor the simple adage, "moderation in all things," as in a little ice cream is fine, but a gallon (3.8 L) a day is not advised.

The same wisdom applies for media. Each family has its own goal for how much screen time is ideal, and those limits will certainly ebb and flow with time and circumstances. Many families choose to strictly limit media with young children and then gradually allow more time as the child grows older. Listen to your inner wisdom and don't be distracted by what other families do. Find your right path and then work your way in that direction.

THE IMPORTANCE OF UNSCHEDULED TIME

Many children today have a full calendar, from morning until night, year-round. School and after-school activities, homework, sports, and other obligations create a free time deficit in many kids' lives. Overscheduling can quickly overwhelm their innate sense of wonder, play, and curiosity.

Mindfully allow for unscheduled free time in your child's week. In the space you create, they will have the opportunity to explore, grow, and flourish.

I'M BORED!

Okay, so not all kids know how to handle unscheduled time with perfect grace. Enduring the cry of "I'm bored!" is a summer vacation rite of passage for many parents, as kids learn how to navigate a more open schedule.

I believe, however, that for most kids, boredom is not inherently bad. If we provide our children with a rich environment and the freedom to explore, good things will blossom from the discomfort of this unfamiliar freedom. When my own kids tell me they are bored, I say, "How wonderful! I can't wait to see what you're about to create." They're rarely thrilled with my reply, but every time it has turned out to be true.

Know your child, their needs, and their limits; practice patience; and provide space and time for exploration. Give them access to resources for the projects in this book and provide a simple, open-ended "unplugged play zone" to encourage exploration. Then, watch their boredom transform into something truly magical.

OFFLINE FOR ALL (MODELING FOR YOUR KIDS)

If your goal is for your child to spend more time offline and engaged in the physical or natural world, it's helpful (dare I say *vital*) that you do the same. Model for your kids the actions you want them to take, whether it's spending more time outdoors, offline, or creating. Trust me, they'll notice. And, they'll follow your lead.

Remember, even as adults, unplugging needn't be a drag! Think of it as a pause, a challenge, and a much-needed reset for yourself and your children. When you discover how much fun you're having offline, doing it more often will become a breeze.

IN THIS TOGETHER

Parents are as overextended as children in the modern world, so it's tempting to send our kids off to play, create, or explore without us. But spending time unplugged *and* together is where the magic happens.

Commit yourself to just five minutes of unplugged playtime with the child in your life today and every day, whether outside or at the craft table. You can do five minutes, and I'll wager you'll end up wanting more. Your kids will delight in sharing this journey with you, and you're sure to discover a new craft, recipe, or activity to love along the way.

MAKING SPACE FOR UNPLUGGED PLAY

Providing your child with materials and resources for a rich and satisfying unplugged

EMBRACING IMPERFECTION

No one is perfect! No kid or grown-up has it all together, and none of us are rocking this unplugged family fun gig with picture-perfect grace. Keep that in mind as you inch your way toward more offline quality time with your family.

There will almost certainly be off days and flops, conflicts and backslides. And that's okay. The only goals here are those that you set for yourself, and tomorrow is the perfect time to start anew.

experience needn't be difficult (or costly). Don't feel limited by the size of your home. Even in a tiny house, efficiency apartment, or RV on the road, there's space to carve out for creative, offline play. A shoebox of craft supplies tucked into a cupboard, under your child's bed, or on a bookshelf is all you need.

THE SPACE

Provide your child with a space where they can make messes and create magic. Choose a site that is easy to keep clean. Avoid carpeted floors, upholstered chairs, and other hard-to-clean or delicate surfaces.

Your creative space might be a designated craft table in the corner of the kitchen or your regular kitchen table or countertop. If possible, refrain from setting up the crafting space in your child's bedroom or other out-of-the-way room as this journey is meant to be shared. Keep a couple of drop cloths or old tablecloths handy for projects that can get messy.

THE SUPPLIES

The creative supplies listed here are a starting point for what you might choose to include. Let your child's interests lead the way and then stock up on whatever they're most inspired to use.

Start by looking through your own desk drawers before buying new. Then, check your local thrift store's craft area for affordable secondhand supplies. See the Resources section (page 137) for where to buy some of the more uncommon items on the list. Remember, more isn't always better. Keep it simple to encourage your child to play and explore without feeling overwhelmed. Minimalism for the win!

THE BASICS

* 6 to 24 colored pencils
* A small set of watercolor paints or acrylic paints
* A variety of paper (watercolor, colored, drawing, etc.)
* 1 pair of scissors
* Craft glue

FUN-TO-HAVE EXTRAS

* Wooden peg dolls
* Acorn caps
* Wool felt
* Wool roving
* Needle and thread
* Embroidery floss
* Scrap fabric
* Chenille sticks or pipe cleaners
* Wire cutters
* Scrap wood and fasteners

STEWARDSHIP

In each chapter that follows, there are simple stewardship activities. I believe fostering a love of the natural world and a desire to do our part to protect it is one of the important jobs we have as parents and mentors. From picking up litter to planting trees to feeding birds, we can all pitch in to make the world a healthier and more beautiful place.

A NOTE ABOUT SAFETY

This book includes a variety of projects designed for families with children of all ages. Some crafts or recipes involve the use of knives, pliers, stoves, ovens, candles, campfires, and other mishaps waiting to happen. Although your kids will learn how to use these tools safely when the time is right, for safety's sake, your close supervision and assistance of younger children is expected. Besides, it's so much more fun to create side by side with the kids in your life. By keeping an eye on things, you also get to join in the fun!

DARK AND LIGHT IN BALANCE

From winter solstice until the spring equinox, days gradually grow longer until dark and light are in balance again. On the day of the spring equinox, the entire world experiences roughly twelve hours of daylight and twelve hours of darkness. This light-dark balance happens only two times each year—once in spring and once in fall—when the sun is directly over the equator.

SPRING

SPRING EQUINOX: THE WORLD AWAKENS!
➤ **March 21** in the northern hemisphere
➤ **September 23** in the southern hemisphere

In parts of the world where the winters are long and cold, spring's return is greeted with enthusiasm. This warm relief from an icy, dark season arrives in melting snow, bursting buds, and baby animals of every sort. Even if you live somewhere warmer, springtime still probably means flowers in the garden, birdsong in the trees, or soft green grass beneath your feet. What does spring feel like in your neighborhood?

BABIES, BUDS, AND BLOOMS
As Earth moves slowly from winter into spring, the longer, warmer days stir an awakening in plants and animals alike. For many animals, spring means it's time to raise their young, while food is abundant. The longer days coax hibernating animals from their winter sleep and lure them out into the sunshine once more. Temperatures are mild, making survival that much easier for wildlife. Migratory birds return from their winter retreat and many species begin to build nests, lay eggs, and raise chicks.

In plants, longer days cause buds to swell, as leaves and flowers begin to form beneath protective bud scales. This often begins in late winter, while snow still blankets the ground in some regions, triggered by lengthening days (despite the cold). It's also the time of year when many humans begin thinking of the season ahead and planting their gardens for a supply of fresh vegetables and flowers in the weeks and months to come.

In the colder climates on Earth, above-freezing springtime temperatures trigger the sap to rise in certain trees. This mineral- and nutrient-dense liquid travels from the roots of the tree to its outermost branches, bringing needed energy to developing buds and awakening limbs. This sap can be harvested from maple trees during the brief window between winter and spring and boiled down into sweet, delicious syrup. It's one of my family's favorite springtime traditions! Many of our other favorite springtime traditions are found on the pages that follow.

SUITABLE SPECIES

Force blooms from any of the following species or experiment with other flowering trees and bushes from your own yard:

Almond
Apple
Azalea
Cherry
Crab apple
Forsythia
Horse chestnut
Lilac

Magnolia
Pear
Plum
Pussy willow
Serviceberry
Spirea
Witch hazel

BRANCHES IN BLOOM

Sometimes, we're ready for spring before winter has properly moved on. But by snipping a few branches from a dormant flowering tree or shrub, we can encourage the season's blooms to emerge in our homes a few weeks early. Known as "forcing" blooms, this simple process allows us to welcome a bit of springtime magic into our homes even before the chilly winter world has melted away.

SUPPLIES

* Approximately 1 cup (235 ml) of river stones or marbles (optional)
* Stable Mason jar or vase
* Water, to fill the jar or vase
* Hand pruners or utility knife
* A few 12- to 18-inch (30.5 to 46 cm) branches from a flowering tree or shrub (see list at left)

ACTIVE TIME: under 15 minutes

TOTAL TIME: 2 to 4 weeks

INSTRUCTIONS

1. Carefully place your marbles or river stones (if using) in the bottom of your Mason jar. This will help stabilize your jar. Fill the jar with room-temperature water and set aside.

2. Cut a few branches from a flowering tree or shrub in your yard. Select branches that have plenty of plump flower buds. If you don't have access to a species on the list at left, do a bit of research to see if your flowering shrub is suitable. Make sure you choose a species that's just a month or two from its usual blooming time for best results.

3. Use your pruner or utility knife to carefully cut the base of each branch at a sharp angle. This will allow your branch to take up plenty of water and encourage beautiful blooms.

4. Place the freshly cut branches in the water-filled jar and place the jar in indirect sunlight for 2 to 4 weeks until the buds begin to open. (The amount of time it takes to force blooms will vary by species and time of year!)

5. Refresh the water as needed throughout the flowering process. Soon, you'll notice the buds beginning to grow plumper and then erupt in colorful blooms. Display your jar of blooms until they begin to wilt and then discard them.

NOTE

This activity is suitable for late winter or early spring, after the plants have experienced a minimum of six weeks of cold.

SIGNS OF SPRING SCAVENGER HUNT

Is spring truly here? Head outside and see how many items you can find from the list below. You'll have to use most of your senses to check off the sights, sounds, and smells of spring.

Not all neighborhoods will be host to everything on the list, but a few items from the list are sure to be found on your block or in the skies overhead! If desired, make a photocopy of the list for each member of your family. Or, take your book with you and head outside!

* Buds on trees or shrubs
* Puddles
* An insect of any kind
* Migrating waterfowl
* Birdsong in the air
* Tadpoles or frog eggs
* A spring flower
* A frog (or frog calls)
* Bird's nest

* Soft, green grass
* The feel of a warm breeze
* Caterpillar
* Butterfly or moth
* Baby leaves
* Mud
* Rain clouds
* A tree in bloom
* The smell of coming rain

BEDDING FOR THE BIRDS

Providing nesting materials for the birds is a simple way to welcome spring and help our feathered friends at the same time. Tuck safe bird nesting supplies into the crotch of a tree in your yard, drape between pickets on a fence, or fill a clean wire suet container with nesting supplies and hang it near a window. Then, watch closely as local birds come to gather what they need to make their nests.

SUPPLIES

- ❋ Long strips of grass
- ❋ Cattail fluff
- ❋ Natural, undyed moss
- ❋ Strips of tree bark (gathered from dead, downed trees)
- ❋ Small twigs
- ❋ Tufts of clean, dry pet hair
- ❋ Dried leaves

TIME: under 30 minutes

INSTRUCTIONS

Gather your bedding materials on walks in winter and spring. Then, place them outside for the birds using the suggestions above.

WHAT TO AVOID

Do not provide birds with human hair, string, yarn, or twine, which can tangle around a bird's legs and cause injuries. Avoid dryer lint and any synthetic nesting materials, which may create an unhealthy nest for baby birds or attract moisture or predators. Pet hair from animals that have been treated with flea and tick repellents should also be avoided, and avoid plant material from areas that have been treated with pesticides or herbicides, which can sicken birds.

LILAC SODA SYRUP

Lilac season is fleeting. Capture the delicate sweetness of this garden favorite with this delightful fizzy drink. Delicately purple and downright delicious, it's one snazzy, springtime sip.

INGREDIENTS

* ✳ 4 or 5 large lilac flower clusters (to yield 1½ cups [about 50 g] blooms, removed from the stems)
* ✳ 1 cup (235 ml) water
* ✳ 12 fresh or frozen blueberries (optional, for color)
* ✳ ⅔ cup (230 g) honey or ¾ cup (150 g) sugar

TIME: under 20 minutes

YIELD: 1 cup (235 ml) soda syrup

INSTRUCTIONS

1. Harvest the lilacs on the same day you plan to make your syrup. Pick blooms after the morning dew has dried but before the heat of the day sets in. Choose clusters that are made up of mostly open flowers and avoid those with flowers tinged with brown, already past their prime (these spent flowers will taint the flavor of your finished syrup).

2. Pluck the flowers off the stems, removing as much green as possible. Discard the stems.

3. In a medium-size pot over high heat, bring the water to a boil.

4. Remove the water from the heat and stir in the lilac flowers and blueberries (if using). Cover the pot and let steep for 15 minutes.

5. Stir in the honey or sugar, stirring well to combine. Cover the pot and continue steeping for about 1 hour more or until the soda syrup has cooled to room temperature.

6. Pour the syrup through a fine-mesh strainer, pressing on the solids to extract as much syrup as possible. Compost or discard the solids.

7. Transfer the soda syrup to a clean glass bottle or jar and label with the contents and date.

8. Lilac soda syrup will keep refrigerated in an airtight container for up to 1 week and can be frozen for 1 year.

TO USE

In a tall glass, stir together 3 tablespoons (45 ml) syrup with 1 cup (240 ml) cold carbonated water. Adjust proportions as desired and serve over ice.

NOTE

Every lilac hedge has its own unique flavor, so if you have more than one to harvest from, nibble a flower from each before you decide which has the best flavor. Purple bushes are often most flavorful; whereas, white lilacs tend to be more bitter or bland.

NEIGHBORHOOD BOUQUET SURPRISES

May Day bouquets were once a common way to celebrate spring's arrival and spread a little cheer around the neighborhood on the first of May. As fun to make and give as they are to receive, it's a tradition that's worthy of a comeback. With that in mind, my kids and I deliver them to our neighbors (in secret!) every year.

Stealthily delivered to friends' and neighbors' doors on the first morning of May, these bouquets deliver smiles all around. But you don't need be tied to May 1. Any spring day is the perfect time for a secret flower delivery!

SUPPLIES

* Work gloves
* 1 empty steel can per bouquet (Experiment with different sizes. The ones here are standard 15-ounce [440 ml] soup cans, but tiny tomato paste cans are delightful as well!)
* Fine point permanent marker
* 1 piece scrap lumber sized to fit snugly inside your steel can (A suitably sized downed tree branch or piece of firewood is a great choice, if available, or use dimensional [precut to size] lumber.)
* Hammer
* Large, sturdy nail
* Scissors
* Kitchen string, twine, or ribbon
* Water
* Small handful fresh spring flowers and greens for each bouquet—violets, dandelions, and other backyard volunteers are as lovely as purchased flowers.

TIME: under 45 minutes, plus time to deliver bouquets

INSTRUCTIONS

PART 1: PREPARE YOUR CANS

1. Wash the steel cans with a long-handled brush if needed. (Do not wash with a cloth or sponge, as inserting your hand in the can could result in cuts.) Rinse well.

2. Dry the outside of each can.

NOTE

The cut edge of a steel can may be very sharp! Wear work gloves while assembling your bouquets to prevent cuts. For greater safety, file the edges of your cans with a metal file (while wearing work gloves), if desired.

(continued)

Pictured opposite: marsh marigolds, violet leaves, daylily leaves, and wild catnip sprigs

PART 2: ATTACH STRING HANDLES

1. Locate the seam running from rim to rim on one of your cans. Place this seam toward the back.

2. Using your permanent marker, place a small dot just below the rim at each side, halfway around the can from the back seam and the center front. To help you place your dots in the proper location, visualize the top of the soup can as a clock. The seam is at 12:00, and your dots should be placed at 3:00 and 9:00.

3. Wearing your work gloves, carefully place a piece of scrap lumber inside the soup can.

4. Using a hammer and a sturdy nail, pierce a hole beneath the can rim at each of your two dots. Rotate the nail to make the hole a bit larger if desired. Carefully remove the scrap lumber. Repeat on all cans. If your can bends a little while hammering, don't despair. Just give it a squeeze and it should go more or less back into shape. Once filled with flowers, any imperfections will not be noticed.

5. Cut an 18-inch (46 cm) length of kitchen twine. Tie a double knot at one end of your twine, large enough not to pass through the hole you just made. Carefully feed the long end of the string in through the hole on one side of the can and then out through the hole on the other side.

6. Tie a second knot to secure your string handle on your can. Give the string a little tug to make sure your knots are large enough not to pass through the holes. If they pull through, tie an additional knot over the top of the previous ones.

PART 3: ASSEMBLE YOUR BOUQUETS

1. After the handles are secured, fill each can halfway with water.

2. Arrange the flowers and greens in each can, being mindful to keep the can seams toward the back.

3. Place your cans in a stable basket or box before setting out for delivery.

PART 4: SECRET DELIVERY

Head out with a grown-up to deliver your bouquet surprises to friends and neighbors. Knock on the door and wish them a happy spring or (our favorite and the traditional way to deliver a May basket) secretly hang the bouquets from a doorknob or fence and then dash away unseen. Your friends will find the flowers after you've gone home and wonder who delivered the spring magic to their front door!

HERBAL FIRST-AID BALM

A homemade first-aid balm is easy to make! It's also a welcome comfort when scrapes and tumbles happen while exploring. Tuck a tin in your pocket or pack when you head out to the parks, fields, or forests around your neighborhood. To make our first-aid balm, we'll start by infusing herbs in oil. Then, we'll create a balm using our infused oil and beeswax. Either dried or fresh herbs can be used.

PART 1: INFUSE YOUR OIL

INGREDIENTS AND SUPPLIES

* ½ cup fresh herbs or 3 tablespoons dried (weight varies; suggestions follow)
* 1 cup (235 ml) organic olive oil or sunflower oil
* Double boiler or two stainless steel or glass cooking pots that can be nested, one inside the other
* Metal mixing spoon
* Glass jar with lid (optional)

TIME: about 1 hour

YIELD: 5 ounces (140 g) balm

INSTRUCTIONS

1. If using fresh herbs, harvest them in the morning on a rainless day, after the dew has dried. Pick over your herbs and remove any garden debris and then allow your plants to wilt for 24 hours to reduce surface moisture. (Do not wash, which will add too much moisture and can cause your infusion to spoil.)

2. Coarsely chop your wilted, fresh herbs or gently crumble the dried herbs and then place them in a small glass or steel saucepan. Cover the herbs with oil. Place the pan in a slightly larger pot that is partially filled with water, creating a double boiler.

3. Gently warm the double boiler over low heat until the water simmers and the oil and herb mixture is warm, about 10 to 15 minutes.

4. Cover the pan and remove it from heat, leaving the double boiler assembled. Let cool to room temperature. Allow to infuse overnight.

5. Return your double boiler to the heat and gently rewarm the mixture. When the water is just below a simmer, remove the inner pot and let cool slightly. When just warm to the touch, dry off the outside of the pot and then strain your oil through a clean, dry piece of cheesecloth, squeezing to extract as much goodness as possible from the herbs. Compost or discard the herbs.

6. Use your oil to make the first-aid balm or store in a clean, dry labeled jar for up to 1 year.

ACTIVE TIME: under 20 minutes

TOTAL TIME: 24 to 48 hours

NOTE

Dried herbs can be purchased at most natural food stores, or you can grow your own! (Some, like common plantain, are probably already growing in your neighborhood.)

(continued)

PART 2: MAKE YOUR BALMS

INGREDIENTS AND SUPPLIES

* ½ cup (120 ml) herb-infused oil (recipe precedes)
* 1 tablespoon plus 1 teaspoon (19 g) grated beeswax
* Double boiler or two stainless steel or glass cooking pots that can be nested, one inside the other
* Metal mixing spoon
* Small glass jars or steel tins, for finished balm

TIME: under 20 minutes

INSTRUCTIONS

1. In a small stainless steel or glass pan, combine the herb-infused oil and beeswax. Place the pan in a slightly larger pot that is partially filled with water, creating a double boiler.

2. Warm over low heat until the water begins to simmer and the beeswax melts.

3. Remove from the heat and let cool slightly. Remove the inner pot from the double boiler and dry off the outside of the pot. Carefully pour the balm into small glass jars or metal tins. If the balm hardens during pouring, simply rewarm it over very low heat.

4. Let the balm sit, undisturbed, until cool and then cover and label it. Store in a cool, dry place for up to 1 year.

TO USE

Apply the balm liberally, as needed, to bumps and bruises, skinned knees, and shallow cuts. Discontinue use if irritation develops.

BENEFICIAL HERBS

Infuse your balm with any (or all) of the first-aid herbs listed here. If you are foraging your herbs, only harvest them from areas free of chemical spray, car traffic, and pet waste and only harvest herbs that you are 100 percent certain of their identity.

* **Calendula flowers:** Wonderful for any irritated skin, including rashes, cuts, scrapes, and sunburn
* **Chamomile:** Good for red or irritated skin
* **Plantain leaf:** A favorite herb for treating bee stings and slivers
* **Yarrow flower and leaf:** Great for soothing scrapes and shallow cuts

TREE RING TALES

Have you ever noticed the growth rings in a tree stump or piece of firewood? Those rings tell a story of abundant sunshine and rain, hard winters, and cold springs. Each ring represents a year of growth for that tree, beginning with the lighter, broader band. This band grew when rain and sunlight were abundant. As summer winds to a close, the tree's growth slows, until autumn, when leaves fall and growth stops for the season. As the tree shuts down its growth for the year, the rings become dense, dark, and tight, represented by a thin, dark ring. The tree rests until spring, when long days cause another ring of fast growth and another light line in the tree's wood.

PLANTING TREES

There's a saying about tree planting that goes, "The best time to plant a tree was 100 years ago. The second best time is today." And because none of us were here 100 years ago, shovel in hand, it simply means today is the perfect time to plant a tree. It's a gift to ourselves and our homes, our neighborhoods, and our planet.

Planting trees provides habit for wildlife, shade for our homes, and oxygen for the Earth. Trees also remove carbon from the atmosphere, something that's great for the environment. Even if your family doesn't own land, you can still help by joining tree planting efforts in your community (see the Resources section, page 137, for ideas on how to get involved). And in 1 year or 100, there will be no question that today was the perfect day to plant a tree.

SUPPLIES

* Shovel
* 1 or more bare-root or potted trees
* Water

TIME: under 30 minutes per tree

INSTRUCTIONS

1. Two weeks before you plan to plant, ask an adult to contact the service in your area that flags buried power lines (sometimes called "Digger's Hotline"). This free service is necessary for safety before you dig—do not skip this life-saving step!

2. After any buried wires have been flagged, choose a suitable planting location. Unless your tree is a dwarf variety, plant a minimum of 20 feet (6 m) from houses and other buildings and at least 50 feet (15.3 m) from overhead power lines.

3. Dig a hole twice the size of your tree's root ball. Loosen the dirt in the hole.

4. Unwrap your tree or gently remove it from the pot. Place it root-first into the hole. If you can do so without damaging them, carefully separate the larger roots, spreading them apart in the hole.

5. Shovel the soil you removed back into the hole and carefully spread it around the tree roots.

6. Replace all the soil and then gently press down to remove air pockets.

7. Immediately after planting, water your tree slowly and deeply.

8. Every two days (more in dry climates, less if it rains), deeply water your tree to keep it healthy. After it is well established, you can water less frequently, but keep watering throughout the first growing season.

CANDIED VIOLETS

Did you know that wild violet flowers (Viola ssp.) are edible? Purchase some from your local farmers' market or if you are able to ID them with certainty, gather a few from a clean, out-of-the-way corner of your yard or garden. If wild violets aren't available, ask your grocer or farmer for other suitable, edible species. Then, try your hand at making candied blossoms. Use your sugared blooms to decorate cakes, cookies, and other springtime treats.

INGREDIENTS AND SUPPLIES

- ✳ **12 or more edible violets or other edible, organic flowers**
- ✳ **1 tablespoon (8 g) cornstarch**
- ✳ **1 tablespoon plus 1 teaspoon (20 ml) water**
- ✳ **Caster sugar, for decorating (See sidebar for instructions to make your own from regular granulated sugar.)**
- ✳ **1 small paintbrush, reserved for food use only**
- ✳ **Baking sheet lined with parchment paper**
- ✳ **Glass jar with lid (optional)**

TIME: under 1 hour

YIELD: 12 candied flowers

NOTE

Not all flowers are edible. Indeed, many can make you ill if consumed. Edible species include wild violets (from the viola family), organic roses, lilacs, and chamomile. Only use flowers that you are 100 percent certain are edible and always check with a knowledgeable grown-up before eating plants from the wild. Some flowers contain poison that can make you very sick, so don't take chances. Never substitute inedible African violets (Saintpaulia species) for edible wild viola flowers. Unlike wild violets, African violets are not edible and can make you ill. Be sure to use only organically-grown flowers, raised without chemical sprays or synthetic pesticides.

INSTRUCTIONS

1. Harvest flowers after the morning dew has dried, leaving 2 inches (5 cm) or more of stem attached to the flower. Choose only flowers that are free of browning and dirt and are growing away from chemical sprays, roads, and pet waste—and be sure to leave plenty for the bees!

2. Back inside, pick over your harvest to remove any damaged blooms or dirty flowers. *Do not wash the flowers.*

3. In a small bowl, whisk the cornstarch and water until the cornstarch dissolves. The mixture should be thick.

4. Holding one flower by the stem, carefully paint the cornstarch mixture onto both sides of each petal. Gently separate the petals, if needed, to fully coat the entire flower.

5. Sprinkle the sugar over the freshly painted flower and then set it on the parchment-lined baking sheet to dry. Repeat with the remaining flowers. In humid climates, you can dry the flowers in a food dehydrator or oven set to the lowest possible temperature (below 150°F, or 65.5°C) until crisp and dry (about 3 hours). In dry climates, dry the flowers at room temperature for 2 to 3 days until fully dried and crisp. Drying time will vary by humidity, so allow plenty of time for your flowers to dehydrate until thoroughly crisp.

6. Store the dried flowers in layers, separated by waxed paper, in a tightly sealed glass jar for up to 6 months.

TO USE

Place your candied violets on homemade treats like cupcakes, cookies, chocolates, and brownies. (Allow your baked goods to cool completely before applying the flowers to prevent them from becoming soft.) Candied flowers can be held in place with a small dab of frosting or a drizzle of icing, if desired.

HOMEMADE CASTER SUGAR

Caster sugar is like ordinary granulated sugar, but with a smaller grain size. (It's not the same as powdered sugar, which is light and powdery, instead of granular.) If you can't find caster sugar at the market, make your own!

Place ½ cup (100 g) granulated sugar in a food processor. Cover the food processor with a kitchen towel to contain the sugar dust and run the machine on high for 1 to 2 minutes or until the sugar is finely ground. Wait for the dust to settle before removing the cover and then proceed with the recipe.

WILD SPRING SALAD WITH HONEY BALSAMIC VINAIGRETTE

When it's time to make a salad, most of us head to the farmers' market, garden, or grocery store. But maybe the backyard is an even better place to begin! Wild spring greens are tender, tasty, and nutritious. And as my favorite herbalist, Rosemary Gladstar, says, eating wild greens makes each of us a little wilder as well! Are you adventurous enough to try a wild salad?

HONEY BALSAMIC VINAIGRETTE INGREDIENTS

* ¼ cup (60 ml) olive oil
* 2 tablespoons (28 ml) apple cider vinegar
* 1 tablespoon (15 ml) balsamic vinegar
* 1 tablespoon (20 g) raw honey
* ½ teaspoon minced garlic
* 1 teaspoon dried thyme
* Pinch salt
* Few grinds black pepper

WILD SPRING SALAD INGREDIENTS

* 2 to 3 cups (110 to 165 g) freshly foraged wild greens (See suggestions following.)
* 4 to 6 cups (220 to 330 g) fresh baby greens or lettuce of choice
* Handful fresh chive blossoms, nasturtiums, or other edible flowers

TIME: Under 20 minutes

YIELD: 6 servings; makes 1 cup (235 ml) salad dressing

INSTRUCTIONS

1. To make the Honey Balsamic Vinaigrette: In a pint-size (473 ml) Mason jar or bowl, combine all the vinaigrette ingredients. Cover the jar with a tight fitting lid and shake well, or whisk, until thoroughly combined. Set aside.

2. To make the Wild Spring Salad: Pick over the wild greens, removing any garden debris, and tear into bite-size pieces. Tear the lettuce into bite-size pieces as well. In a large colander, combine the greens and lettuce, rinse with cold water, and spin or gently blot dry. Transfer to a salad bowl.

3. Sprinkle in the chive blossoms.

4. Serve the salad and pass the vinaigrette at the table or dress the salad just before serving.

5. Leftover vinaigrette can be refrigerated sealed tightly in the jar for up to 3 weeks.

NATURE NOTES

Many common backyard "weeds" are actually tasty, nutritious salad greens! Pictured here (clockwise from the bowl at center/bottom): giant chickweed, cleavers, plantain leaf, field mallow, dandelion flowers, violet leaf and flowers, and dandelion leaf. For safety's sake, only forage wild greens that you are 100 percent certain of their identity. Have a knowledgeable adult double check your harvest before eating. And forage only in areas that are free of pet waste, chemical sprays, and nearby car traffic.

ROSE AND CARDAMOM HERBAL TEA

This tea is warm, floral, and lifts the heart—just like springtime! If you wish, make a big batch and package up the extras in repurposed jam jars. If you host a springtime party (see next page), make a big batch and attach a tag with ingredients and brewing instructions and send one home with each guest.

INGREDIENTS

* ✳ 3 tablespoons (4.5 g) dried organic rose petals
* ✳ 2 tablespoons (12 g) dried organic calendula flowers
* ✳ 2 tablespoons (15 g) dried organic raspberry leaf
* ✳ 2 tablespoons (12 g) rooibos tea
* ✳ 1 tablespoon (6 g) cardamom seeds or cracked green cardamom pods

TIME: under 20 minutes

YIELD: a generous ⅔ cup (50 g) dry tea blend

INSTRUCTIONS

1. In a clean, dry medium-size bowl, combine all the ingredients.

2. Crush any large leaves or flowers between your fingers, if necessary.

3. Stir well to combine. Transfer to a glass storage jar, cover the jar, and label and date the tea blend. Keep in a cool, dry place for up to 1 year.

TO USE

Measure 1 tablespoon (about 6 g) of tea blend into a tea strainer or directly into a teapot. Pour 2 cups (475 ml) of just-boiled water over the tea, cover, and let steep for 5 to 10 minutes. Strain, cool, and serve. If you like, add a drop of honey (avoid honey for children under 1 year of age) and a splash of milk or cream.

NOTE

Choose only organic rose petals and other floral ingredients. Roses sold in flower shops are often treated with chemicals that make them unsafe to consume.

A SPRINGTIME FLOWER FESTIVAL

Gather with friends and family to celebrate the return of warmer days. This simple tea party is equally delightful shared with just one friend as it is with a garden-full of friends.

Enjoy any or all of the spring festivities following or create your own celebration with the recipes and projects found in this chapter.

HOLIDAY: Spring Equinox

LOCATION: Celebrate in your backyard or a neighborhood park. In the event of rain, move the party indoors to your kitchen or dining room.

DECORATIONS: Flower Crowns (page 43) and wildflower bouquets

FOOD AND DRINK: Rose and Cardamom Herbal Tea (page 35), Wild and Tame Tea Sandwiches (page 38), and Violet Shortbread Cookies (page 41)

ACTIVITIES AND PARTY FAVORS: Flower Crowns (page 43) and Teacup Fairy Gardens (page 44)

WILD AND TAME TEA SANDWICHES

Teatime is notoriously polite and civilized. So, let's break with tradition and go a little wild! Made with a delicious, vibrant, absolutely scrumptious herbal sandwich spread and held together with leafy apple twigs, I think these sandwiches make teatime that much more wildly delightful. Make your spread with whatever wild greens you have on hand from your yard or garden or head to the farmers' market to buy bitter dandelion greens, spicy arugula, or mild spinach.

WILD AND TAME SANDWICH SPREAD INGREDIENTS

* ¼ cup (35 g) pine nuts or walnuts
* 2 cups (110 g) fresh mild greens (chickweed, violet leaf, spinach, or parsley), loosely packed
* 1 cup (55 g) assorted fresh flavorful greens (dandelion leaves, garlic mustard, lamb's quarters, arugula, or watercress), loosely packed
* ½ cup (12 g) fresh basil, loosely packed
* ¾ cup (175 ml) olive oil
* 2 large cloves garlic, peeled (Omit if using garlic mustard greens.)
* ⅛ teaspoon salt, plus more as needed

TIME: under 30 minutes, including making the sandwich spread

YIELD: 8 small tea sandwiches; 2 cups (about 400 g) spread

TEA SANDWICH INGREDIENTS

* 8 small, fresh apple branches, with young leaves or flowers still attached (substitute birch, maple, or oak twigs, if desired) about the diameter of a wooden kitchen skewer or purchased sandwich picks
* 8 pieces sandwich bread (white, soft whole wheat, or gluten free)
* 4 tablespoons (55 g) butter, at room temperature, plus more as needed
* Mild cheese slices of choice (I love provolone, Jack, or spreadable goat cheese.)
* Sliced cooked, chilled chicken
* Sliced fresh tomatoes (optional)

INSTRUCTIONS

1. To make the Wild and Tame Sandwich Spread: In a dry skillet over medium heat, toast the pine nuts, stirring constantly, until the nuts begin to darken in areas and smell fragrant. Set aside to cool.

2. Pick over the mild and flavorful greens and remove any garden debris or coarse stems. Transfer to a blender or food processor and add the basil, pine nuts, olive oil, garlic, and salt. Chop or purée until fairly smooth, stopping to scrape down the sides frequently. Taste and add additional salt, if desired. This spread will keep for 3 to 5 days, covered, in the refrigerator.

3. To make the Tea Sandwiches: Using a utility knife, cut one end of each apple branch to a point.

4. Cut off the crusts from the bread slices and then cut each slice in half diagonally. Spread half the bread triangles with Wild and Tame Sandwich Spread. Spread the other half with butter.

5. Layer each piece of buttered bread with cheese, chicken, and tomato (if using) and then top with a sandwich spread slice.

6. Pierce with an apple branch skewer and serve.

STORAGE

For longer storage of the sandwich spread, place heaping tablespoon-size (15 ml) portions of the spread onto a baking sheet. (I use a mini-ice cream scoop, but an everyday spoon will work as well.) Place the sheet into the freezer. When the sandwich spread is frozen, remove the scoops from the tray with a thin spatula and transfer to a storage container or freezer-safe zip-top bag. You can also freeze the sandwich spread in an ice cube tray. Label, date, and freeze for up to 1 year. When needed, remove and thaw the sandwich spread pucks.

VIOLET SHORTBREAD COOKIES

What could be more delightful than homemade shortbread cookies? Why, decorating them with edible flowers, of course! I use fresh wild violets and Candied Violets (page 30) for my cookies, but you could top yours with other edible flowers from your local farmers' market. Gluten-free and vegan variations are included.

INGREDIENTS

- ❋ ½ cup (112 g) unsalted butter, at room temperature, or a vegan butter substitute
- ❋ ¼ cup (80 g) maple syrup
- ❋ Zest of 1 lemon (about 1 packed teaspoon)
- ❋ Pinch salt
- ❋ 1¼ cups (156 g) all-purpose flour or your favorite gluten-free flour blend
- ❋ 16 fresh wild violets, or Candied Violets (page 30), or other edible flower (See Safety Note.)

ACTIVE TIME: under 1 hour
TIME: 3 hours
YIELD: about 16 cookies

INSTRUCTIONS

1. In the bowl of a stand mixer fitted with the paddle attachment or in a large bowl and using an electric hand mixer, beat the butter and maple syrup on medium speed until the syrup is incorporated and butter is fluffy.

2. Add the lemon zest, salt, and flour. Using a wooden spoon, stir until just combined. Do not overmix. Shape the mixture into a log about 9 inches (23 cm) long and 2 inches (5 cm) in diameter. Wrap the log in parchment paper or beeswax cloth and refrigerate for 2 hours or overnight.

3. Preheat the oven to 325°F (170°C, or gas mark 3).

4. Remove the log from the refrigerator and unwrap it. Using a serrated bread knife, slice the dough into ½-inch (1 cm) rounds.

5. If using fresh violets (as shown on the pink plate), place one blossom on each cookie and then gently roll into place with a rolling pin; if using candied violets, apply them after baking and cooling. Arrange the cookies on a baking sheet about 1 inch (2.5 cm) apart.

SAFETY NOTE

Not all flowers are edible, and eating the wrong sort can make you very sick. Check with a knowledgeable grown-up before eating any wild or cultivated flowers.

(continued)

6. Bake for 25 minutes or until cookies are just beginning to turn golden brown. Transfer to a wire rack to cool thoroughly.

7. If using candied violets, drizzle each cooled cookie with royal icing (see below) and then gently place each candied flower over the icing. Let set for 30 minutes, or up to 2 hours, until the icing hardens to hold the flower in place.

ROYAL ICING

In a small bowl, stir together ⅓ cup (40 g) of powdered sugar, 2 teaspoons of milk of your choice, 1 teaspoon of fresh lemon juice, and ¼ teaspoon of vanilla extract until thoroughly combined and smooth. If the icing is too thick, add water, 1 teaspoon at a time, until your desired consistency is reached. If it is too thin, add additional powdered sugar, 1 teaspoon at a time, until your desired consistency is reached.

WEAVING FLOWER CROWNS

Flower crowns are a festive, seasonal delight. And, they're easier to make than you might imagine! This project is based on a simple three-strand braid. Make them ahead for your guests if desired or set out flowers and greenery for your friends to make their own when they arrive.

SUPPLIES

* ❋ An armful of freshly picked herbs or flowers with long, flexible stems
* ❋ Floral wire, yarn, or metal twist-ties

TIME: about 30 minutes

YIELD: 1 crown

INSTRUCTIONS

1. Begin with three sprigs of your chosen herbs or flowers. Lay them close together and parallel on your work surface. Gently braid them for two or three repeats.

2. Lay a fourth sprig over the top of your braid and overlap its stem with the shortest of your three original plants. This will extend the length of the shortest sprig, allowing you to continue working your braid.

3. Continue to add new sprigs every inch or two (2.5 to 5 cm), or as needed, by laying them on top of your work and joining their stems with another in the braid. The shorter your stems, the more often you will have to add new sprigs.

4. Wrap the flower wreath around your head to check for length, holding the loose end tightly to ensure it does not unravel. When your flower or herb braid is long enough to reach around your head with a few inches (about 7.5 cm) of overlap, use a small piece of floral wire to secure the end, in the same manner you would apply a hair tie to braided hair.

5. Use several small pieces of floral wire, yarn, or twist ties to secure the tail behind the decorative braid, forming a crown.

TEACUP FAIRY GARDENS

Ever since I was a child, I've delighted in building fairy houses in the woods and in the garden. I can almost see the fairies there, lazing in their soft mossy beds and leaf blankets and drinking acorn cups of herbal tea.

This project takes fairy house building one step further, creating the fairy garden itself for the wee folk to visit! By layering soil and stones in a vintage teacup and topping with soft, vibrant moss, you can create a home for the fairies right on your own windowsill or table. Add acorns, crystals, paper signposts—Welcome, Fairies!—or other tiny delights as inspiration strikes.

SUPPLIES (PER GUEST)

- ✳ 1 vintage teacup, sugar bowl, Mason jar, or other repurposed vessel, thoroughly washed with soap, rinsed well, and dried
- ✳ Handful pebbles or small stones (¼ inch, or 6 mm, or smaller)
- ✳ Handful activated charcoal chunks (You can find this at garden centers and pet stores for aquariums; see Note.)
- ✳ ¾ cup (weight varies) potting soil
- ✳ Live moss, gathered or purchased (see the Resources section, page 137, for where to buy)
- ✳ Garden gloves
- ✳ Old kitchen spoon
- ✳ Old kitchen butter knife
- ✳ Selection of sea shells, polished stones, crystal points, or other fairy-size treasures
- ✳ Spritz bottle filled with water (to share)

TIME: under 30 minutes

YIELD: 1 fairy garden

INSTRUCTIONS

1. Arrange your supplies on a cloth-covered table or on the ground.

2. Combine equal parts pebbles and charcoal pieces and carefully spoon the mixture into the bottom of your cup, filling it about 1 inch (2.5 cm) deep or roughly one-third the depth of the cup.

3. Spoon potting soil on top of the gravel mix, filling your cup to within ½ inch (1 cm) of the rim.

4. Tear off a piece of moss just larger than the diameter of your teacup or choose several smaller pieces to do the job. Carefully tuck them in around the rim, poking the edge down with an old butter knife for a tidy look.

5. Top the moss with a few treasures like crystal points, polished stones, or wee fairy furniture, nestling them into the moss for stability.

6. Gently water your moss with the spritz bottle and then display your treasure out of direct sunlight.

7. Mist with your spray bottle anytime the moss begins to feel dry, about once a week.

NOTE

Terrarium-making can get messy. Cover your table with an old bed sheet or drop cloth or, better yet, work outside on the grass, porch, or patio.

SOURCING CHARCOAL

The charcoal you'll use in your terrariums isn't the sort sold for backyard barbecues. Find terrarium charcoal at garden centers or stores selling aquarium supplies. The charcoal you want is sold in chunks (resembling crumbly, black gravel) and is called "activated charcoal." It's often sold in fibrous pouches that slide into an aquarium filter, marked "carbon" on the box. Just cut the pouch open with a craft knife or pair of scissors to use.

BE THRIFTY!

There's no need to purchase new teacups or Mason jars for your fairy gardens. Ask permission to scrounge the basement or cupboards for forgotten cups and bowls or hit the local secondhand store, flea market, or neighborhood rummage sales to score some sweet vintage finds. They'll have more character than cups you buy new and because they're repurposed, they're gentle on the Earth.

THE LONGEST DAY

From Spring Equinox until Summer Solstice, the days grow gradually longer. Because of this increase in sunlight, the land warms, stimulating plant growth. On the Summer Solstice, we experience the longest day of the year, while the opposite hemisphere experiences the longest night. This seasonal difference is caused by the tilt of the Earth (called "axial tilt"), which tips half of the planet toward the sun and the other half away from it. Whatever is happening in one hemisphere (Northern or Southern) is the opposite of what is happening on the other side of the globe.

SUMMER

SUMMER SOLSTICE: SEASON OF PLENTY

➤ **June 21** in the Northern Hemisphere

➤ **December 21** in the Southern Hemisphere

As spring unfolds seamlessly into summer, longer and warmer days cause leaves to grow, flowers to bloom, and berries to ripen. The days are abundant—in both food and sunlight—making for an ease of survival not found during leaner times of the year. Humans, too, often delight in the warmth and sunshine of summer, spending more time outdoors exploring and relaxing than during other times of year.

WAKING FROM WINTER'S REST

In this season of plenty, baby animals rapidly grow. Fledgling birds begin to fly and feed on their own, and fawns, fox pups, and other wildlife venture farther from the habitats and dens where they were born. Animals of every age build fat reserves for the leaner days to come when summer's bounty will end.

For people, summer often means a break from school, long sunny days, and more free time than we're used to. For some families, it means tending their backyard garden; whereas for others, it means seeking out activities that go better with the sun.

ROSE PETAL HONEY

Roses in bloom are fleeting, fragrant, and dreamy. Capture the magic of freshly opened roses by infusing their petals in honey. Spread the honey on toast, stir it into tea, or eat it straight off the spoon—and savor the flavor of summer.

INGREDIENTS

❋ 1½ cups (36 g) loosely packed fresh rose petals, removed from the stem, from organically grown roses

❋ 2 cups (680 g) raw honey

TIME: under 20 minutes, not including harvesting time

YIELD: 2 cups (680 g)

INSTRUCTIONS

1. Pick through the petals, removing any debris or insects. Do not wash them.

2. Place the rose petals in a clean, dry 1-pint (473 ml) jar. Cover them with the honey to fill the jar to the shoulders. Using a table knife, gently stir to incorporate the rose petals into the honey. Add more honey, if needed, to fill the jar.

3. Seal the lid and label and date the jar. Place it out of direct sunlight in an out-of-the-way corner of the kitchen to infuse for 4 days to 1 week before transferring the jar to the refrigerator.

NOTE

Only use rose petals from wild roses harvested away from roadways, chemical sprays, and pet waste or purchase organic food-grade blooms.

STRAINING IS OPTIONAL!

There is no need to strain your finished honey, as the petals are edible (and tasty). But if you prefer your honey smooth, simply pour it through a fine-mesh strainer, pressing to extract as much honey from the petals as possible, and refrigerate.

DRAGONFLY WINGS

I've been a bit obsessed with both damselflies and dragonflies since childhood, even raising some from nymphs in an aquarium as a teenager. They are a sure sign of summer, with their glimmering wings slowly fluttering as they perch beside rivers or wetlands. Despite their beauty, dragonflies are fierce, daring, and courageous. Celebrate summer by channeling your inner dragonfly when you tie on a pair of homemade wings.

SUPPLIES

* 4 metal coat hangers or 2 lengths of stiff wire (2½ feet or 75 cm each)
* Wire cutters
* Ruler
* Permanent marker
* Duct tape or other strong utility tape
* 2 pairs retired tights, leggings, or nylons of preferred color
* Scissors
* Hand-sewing needle and thread to match leggings
* 2 lengths of ribbon (4 feet or 120 cm) for straps
* Acrylic paint, for decoration (optional)
* Paintbrush, for decoration (optional)
* White glue, for decoration (optional)
* Small bowl to hold diluted glue, for decoration (optional)
* Fine glitter, for decoration (optional)
* Fabric flowers, for decoration (optional)

TIME: under 2 hours

YIELD: 1 pair of wings

INSTRUCTIONS

1. If using coat hangers for your wing frames, cut off the hanger hook (just below the twisted portion) on both sides. Straighten the two "elbows" to yield a somewhat straight length of wire.

2. Using your ruler, measure 2 inches (5 cm) in from one end of one wire. Mark with your permanent marker. Repeat on the other end. Use this wire as a guide to mark the remaining three wires in the same manner.

3. Bend one wire near one of the markings you just made at a 45-degree angle. Make an oval (or butterfly wing) shape with the wire, ending with another 45-degree angle at the second marking. Your finished shape will be an oval with a stem, the stem being the two ends of the wire. Repeat this process with the remaining 3 wires. If you wish, you may vary the shape of the wings to yield a distinct top and bottom wing appearance, or you can make them all the same shape. (Find inspiration from pictures of dragonflies and damselflies found in a field guide or other nature book.)

(continued)

NATURE NOTES

Did you know that real dragonflies begin life as underwater predators? After hatching out of their aquatic eggs, young dragonflies, called nymphs, emerge as small but mighty hunters. They capture and devour minnows, scuds, and other small aquatic animals. After one to two years spent living (and breathing) underwater, it's time to emerge. They climb up a sprig of growing vegetation or onto a waterside rock and wait. Here they transform inside their exoskeleton (their hard, outer shell) much like a butterfly in a chrysalis and then crack open their exoskeleton and emerge. What a transformation!

4. Tape the two stems of one wing together using duct tape. Repeat on the 3 remaining wings.

5. If using nylons or tights, cut them in half from the crotch to the waistline. If using leggings, cut in the same fashion, following the seam that runs between the crotch and the waist. Reserve the scraps.

6. Slip a leg on each wire wing segment with the ankle toward the wing tip.

7. If using tights or nylons, slide it on until the foot is situated neatly at each wing tip. Trim the fabric at the stem end until just a bit longer than the wing and wing-stem combined and then proceed to step 12.

8. If using leggings, pull a leg onto each wing, until the ankle of the leg extends just beyond the wing tip (with 1 to 2 inches, or 2.5 to 5 cm, of extra length). Trim the fabric at the stem end, just a bit longer than the wing and wing-stem combined.

9. Neatly tuck the fabric under at the wing tip and then secure with a few neat stitches. Knot the thread to secure. Repeat on all wings.

10. Gather excess fabric at the stem-end of each wing, then secure with duct tape over each stem or a few stitches with your needle and thread. Trim away excess fabric that extends beyond the stem end.

11. Lay your 4 wing shapes on the floor, adjusting the shape and positioning until you are pleased with the layout and appearance. Tape together the stems of what will become the left wing pair and the stems of what will become the right wing pair.

12. Next, tape the left and right wing pairs together to make a connected set of 4 wings.

13. Cut a rectangle from the scrap fabric you set aside in step 5 big enough to cover the wing stems and hide any tape or messy stitches (about 2 feet, or 60 cm, long and 2 inches, or 5 cm, wide). Wrap this scrap of fabric around the wings and secure it with a few snug stitches on the side of the wings that will lay against your back.

14. Fold a length of ribbon in the center. Lay the folded section over the wrapped wing stems, as far to the left as you can. Feed through the tails and pull to secure. Repeat with the second ribbon as far to the right as you can. To wear, draw one set of straps over each shoulder. Cross at your chest and tie in a bow at the back or at one hip.

15. Decorate! (Optional): If desired, dress us your wings using glitter and glue, acrylic paint, or fabric flowers. Let your imagination run wild or use pictures of real dragonflies and damselflies for inspiration.

16. If using glitter and glue, dilute 2 parts white glue with 1 part water in a small bowl. Paint glue onto the wings as desired and then sprinkle with glitter. Knock the surplus glitter off onto a tray or newspaper for reuse. Do not rub or the glitter will smear.

LEMON BALM ICE POPS

Lemon balm is related to peppermint and spearmint but it has a bright, fresh, lemony scent and flavor. It's a cinch to grow, and once established, you'll have it for years.

Plant some in a well-drained, out-of-the-way corner of your yard or garden, and you'll find excuses to pick the fragrant, lemony leaves all summer long. My favorite way to enjoy lemon balm? In ice pops, of course! (No lemon balm? Use fresh or dried peppermint, following the variation below.) Fresh herbs are the most flavorful choice for this recipe, but ice pops made from dried herbs are also delicious.

INGREDIENTS

- ✳ 1 cup (96 g) fresh lemon balm leaves or ⅓ cup (8.5 g) dried lemon balm leaves, coarsely chopped
- ✳ 2 cups (475 ml) boiling water
- ✳ 3 tablespoons (60 g) raw honey or maple syrup

ACTIVE TIME: under 15 minutes

TOTAL TIME: 3¼ hours

YIELD: 8 small or 4 large ice pops, depending on the size of your mold

INSTRUCTIONS

1. If desired, rinse the fresh lemon balm with cold water to remove any dirt or garden debris.

2. Place the lemon balm in a teapot or warmed Mason jar. Add the boiling water and loosely cover the container. Let steep for 10 minutes.

3. Strain the liquid through a fine-mesh strainer, squeezing as much liquid as you can from the leaves. Sweeten to taste with honey. Let cool and then transfer to your ice pop molds.

4. Freeze for 3 hours until solid.

VARIATIONS

Mix up your ice pop game with these fun variations!

LEMON BALM & GINGER ICE POPS: Add a 1-inch (2.5 cm) piece of fresh ginger, thinly sliced, to the lemon balm while steeping. Proceed with the recipe as directed.

PEPPERMINT ICE POPS: Substitute fresh peppermint for the lemon balm for a different flavor. Add a few strips of lemon zest to your steeping herbs for even more flavor.

STRAWBERRY & LEMON BALM ICE POPS: Add 1 cup (170 g) chopped fresh strawberries to the steeping water. Steep until the water is cooled and then proceed as directed, straining out and discarding the strawberry pulp with the lemon balm.

BACKYARD CAMPOUT

Sure, state parks and campgrounds can be fun, but if you or a loved one has a yard, that can be even better. Simply set up a tent in the backyard, grab bedding, a flashlight, and a book, and head out for the night! (A campfire, when possible, adds an extra layer of fun, but is by no means necessary for a great campout. Check with local ordinances and talk to your family before setting up for a campfire.)

SUPPLIES

* ❈ Tent
* ❈ Bedding (sleeping bags, bedrolls, pillows, blankets, bedsheets)
* ❈ Flashlight or headlamp
* ❈ Book
* ❈ Games (cards, board games, etc.)
* ❈ Filled water bottle
* ❈ Campfire wood, if a fire pit is available (optional)
* ❈ Simple, eat-outside dinner (optional)
* ❈ Marshmallows or s'more ingredients (cookies or graham crackers, marshmallows, and chocolate; optional)

INSTRUCTIONS

1. Gather your gear and head outside to set up camp for the night.

2. Pitch the tent in an out-of-the-way corner of your yard and then lay out your bedding inside, preparing your sleeping space before darkness falls.

3. If desired, spend the evening outside playing games, sitting around a campfire, or telling stories as night settles in.

4. At bedtime, head into your tent to enjoy books by flashlight. Fall asleep listening to the breeze and other nighttime sounds of your neighborhood.

HOMEMADE ICE CREAM WITH SUMMER BERRIES

Few things delight the entire family more than fresh homemade ice cream! I love every flavor and am constantly finding excuses to make and enjoy a batch. This summertime version is a rich vanilla custard swirled with a fresh, juicy ribbon of berries. Use whichever summer berry you love most or mix it up and combine all your favorites. My family especially loves blueberry, mulberry, and raspberry. (Allergic to milk? No problem! A dairy-free variation follows, as well as a no-churn tip!)

ICE CREAM CUSTARD INGREDIENTS

* ½ vanilla bean, seeds scraped out (seeds and bean reserved), or 1 teaspoon vanilla extract
* 2 cups (475 ml) heavy cream
* 1 cup (235 ml) whole milk
* Zest of 1 lemon
* Pinch salt
* 2 teaspoons grass-fed gelatin powder (optional)
* ½ cup (160 g) raw honey or ⅔ cup (133 g) sugar

BERRY SWIRL INGREDIENTS

* 2 cups (weight varies) berries of choice, whole if small berries (like blueberries), or quartered or cut into eighths if large (like strawberries)
* 2 tablespoons (30 ml) water
* 2 tablespoons (40 g) honey, maple syrup (40g), or sugar (25 g)
* 1 teaspoon fresh lemon juice (from ½ lemon)
* Zest of 1 lemon

ACTIVE TIME: under 30 minutes

TOTAL TIME: under 5 hours

YIELD: 1 quart (about 946 ml)

INSTRUCTIONS
PART 1: PREPARE THE ICE CREAM CUSTARD

1. Place a quart-size (946 ml) freezer-safe storage container in your freezer to chill.

2. Place the vanilla bean seeds and vanilla bean into a medium-size saucepan (if using vanilla extract, wait until step 5) and add the heavy cream, milk, lemon zest, and salt. Warm over medium heat, stirring frequently, until quite hot but below a boil. Remove from the heat.

3. Sprinkle the gelatin (if using) over the surface of the heated cream mixture and then whisk well to combine. If using sugar in place of honey, whisk it in now to combine. Let the custard cool for 15 to 20 minutes until just warm to the touch.

4. If using honey and vanilla extract, whisk in those ingredients now until thoroughly combined. Transfer the custard to a quart-size (946 ml) Mason jar, and refrigerate until thoroughly chilled, a minimum of 4 hours or overnight.

NOTE

Homemade ice cream freezes harder than store-bought, which has air whipped in during freezing. The optional gelatin in the recipe helps keep the ice cream scoopably soft, even straight from the deep freeze. If you choose not to use it, simply let the ice cream sit at room temperature for 5 to 15 minutes to soften before serving.

(continued)

PART 2: MAKE THE FRUIT COMPOTE

In a small saucepan over medium heat, combine the berries, water, honey, lemon juice, and lemon zest. Bring to a simmer, stirring frequently. Cook for 10 to 15 minutes until the berries release their juices and the sauce begins to thicken. Remove the compote from the heat, cool slightly and then transfer to a storage jar. Refrigerate until thoroughly cooled, a minimum of 2 hours.

PART 3: CHURN THE ICE CREAM

1. If gelatin was used, first transfer the custard to a large bowl and whisk until smooth.

2. Transfer either version now to an ice cream maker and churn according to the manufacturer's instructions.

TIP

If you don't own an ice cream maker, transfer your custard to a wide, flat freezer-safe storage container and pop it into the freezer. Freeze for 25 minutes. Remove and whisk well by hand or using an electric hand mixer. Return to the freezer and repeat the whisking every 25 minutes until the custard reaches the consistency of purchased ice cream. Freeze 25 minutes more to set and then enjoy.

PART 4: SWIRL, SET, AND SERVE

When the ice cream is ready, transfer it to your prechilled container, layering ice cream with chilled berry compote. Swirl with a spoon, but don't overmix and then return the ice cream to the freezer to set for 3 hours or overnight. Serve and enjoy!

VARIATIONS

DAIRY-FREE/VEGAN ICE CREAM: Replace the milk and cream with 3 cups (700 ml) full-fat coconut milk. Proceed with the recipe as instructed. Omit the gelatin and use sugar in place of the honey for a vegan version.

BLUEBERRY + BUTTERMILK ICE CREAM: Omit the milk, proceeding with 2 cups (475 ml) of heavy cream only. After chilling the custard base and just before churning, whisk in 1 cup (235 ml) of cold buttermilk or yogurt (230 g) and proceed with the recipe as written. Use blueberries to make the compote.

DOUBLE BERRY SWIRL: Make two half-batches of compote using different berries and swirl them both into the custard before serving.

NATURE EXPLORATION PACK

Having the right gear for whatever unfolds is part of the fun of setting off on a new adventure. A well-stocked nature exploration pack will make it easier to get outside and explore. Snail shells, beetles, and other magic await!

SUPPLIES

* ❋ Backpack
* ❋ Drawstring or resealable bags in a variety of sizes
* ❋ Permanent marker
* ❋ Magnifying glass
* ❋ Binoculars
* ❋ Maps of your favorite hiking trails or parks
* ❋ 1 to 3 field guides (insects, animal tracks, birds, etc.)
* ❋ Bandana
* ❋ First-aid kit
* ❋ Filled reusable water bottle
* ❋ Whistle
* ❋ Small bug net
* ❋ Sketchbook or notebook/nature journal
* ❋ Colored or graphite pencils
* ❋ Bug boxes
* ❋ Small, lightweight trowel

ASSEMBLY TIME: under 15 minutes after supplies have been gathered

YIELD: 1 exploration backpack

INSTRUCTIONS

1. Gather your Nature Exploration Pack supplies.

2. Place small items in resealable bags and label each bag with its contents.

3. Organize your supplies in your backpack in a manner that makes sense to you and is comfortable when worn.

4. After filling, zip your pack closed and try it on. If it's comfortable, you're ready for your next adventure! If your pack feels awkward or heavy, rearrange the contents or remove a few items until you find a comfortable fit.

5. Hit the trails and discover all that's happening just beyond your door!

NOTE

Many of the supplies you need can be found in your kitchen, basement, or garage. Others can be found for pennies at yard sales and thrift shops. Don't get hung up on finding every item on the list. Use it as a jumping off point and add to (or subtract from) your pack as inspiration strikes.

LITTER CLEANUP CHALLENGE

One of my goals each time I head to the beach, the woods, or even down my favorite city streets is to leave the world a bit better than I found it. Often, that means doing my part to clean up what others have left behind.

Litter and trash are everywhere, and it's all too easy just to walk on by. But what would happen if each of us showed the extra care to pick up some litter every time we went outside? The beaches, forests, and neighborhoods we love would be more beautiful and healthier, along with the plants and animals that call them home. Will you join me and challenge yourself to pick up litter when you find it?

SAFETY NOTE

Most litter is dangerous only to the animals who encounter it in their habitats. But some litter can be dangerous to people, too. Never pick up any items you think could harm you. Broken glass, diapers, pet waste, tissues, medical needles, batteries, and other potentially dangerous items should be collected by adults only, so ask for help when necessary.

BUILD A MUD KITCHEN

Ever since my kids were small, our backyard has been host to a busy little mud kitchen, turning out mud pies and chocolates, leaf teas and cocoas, and all manner of messy pretend cuisine. It's such an important piece of our outdoor play landscape, and I can't imagine childhood without it. The supplies to build your own are flexible. Gather any items from the list below or simply use what you have on hand or can source free from friends or neighbors.

SUPPLIES

* Boards
* Cinder blocks or bricks
* Sturdy logs
* Paint
* Tree branches
* Old, small plastic or metal mixing bowls, cooking pots, and baking pans
* Unbreakable picnic plates, pitchers, and other tableware
* A source of soil, sand, leaves, water, and other "ingredients"

TIME: under 2 hours

YIELD: 1 mud kitchen

INSTRUCTIONS

1. Choose a location to set up your mud kitchen—an out-of-the-way location still within view of the house is best.

2. Assemble a sturdy, makeshift "stove" using boards and cinder blocks, bricks, or logs. Paint "burners" on the boards, if desired, or leave them as is for open-ended play. (My daughter nailed a few wooden rectangles in two X shapes to suggest burners on her mud kitchen stove.)

3. Assemble a kitchen counter or shelf for storage and stack with thrifted, unbreakable tableware.

4. Get cooking! Let your imagination run wild. Mix up all manner of baked goods and beverages using whatever you have access to. Serve your creations to a willing parent, pet, or friend for pretend eating. Mmmm! Delicious, messy fun.

5. Clean up your mud kitchen before heading back inside, storing pots and pans upside-down to prevent them from filling with rainwater.

TIP

If you don't have access to an outdoor place for a mud kitchen, try my favorite indoor version—kitchen potions. Ask a grown-up for any expired dry goods, like stale spices or past-date flour, dry beans, etc. Cover a table or other work surface with a drop cloth and lay out cups, pitchers, and spoons. Mix up your pretend creations and serve them to your make-believe guests.

WATERSIDE POTLUCK PARTY

Celebrate the peak of summer with a high summer celebration! Gather with friends and neighbors and indulge in some classic summer potluck fun.

Enjoy any or all of the summer festivities following or create your own celebration with the recipes and projects found in this chapter.

HOLIDAY: Summer Solstice

LOCATION: Gather your friends and family beside a lake, stream, river, or ocean. In a pinch, a backyard wading pool will do!

DECORATIONS: Summer Flower Bunting (page 64)

FOOD AND DRINK: Hibiscus iced tea and potluck offerings of seasonal, local, summertime fare (see page 67)

ACTIVITIES: Blow Giant Bubbles (page 69) and have a Bark-and-Leaf Boat Regatta (page 68)

WHAT'S A POTLUCK?

A potluck is a classic American celebration where each guest brings a dish of food to share and their own picnic dishes for easiest cleanup. Potlucks are a fun way to create a party that's a snap to host and a pleasure to attend.

SUMMER FLOWER BUNTING

Throughout many parts of the world, vibrant flowers are strung together to create festive decorations for home or to wear on your body. In some cultures, these flower strands are considered sacred. From India to Hawaii to Mexico, flower garlands and chains are a sacred and meaningful way to beautify family celebrations.

To dress up your own summer party, why not try your hand at making one? Craft yours from marigolds, like those pictured, or experiment with calendula, zinnias, or other sturdy, substantial blooms. The results are delightful, whatever flowers you choose!

SUPPLIES

* Scissors
* Embroidery floss or other sturdy cotton string
* Wooden beads (optional)
* 40 to 50 sturdy flower heads
* Hand sewing needle that will fit your thread

TIME: under 45 minutes

YIELD: 1 bunting (6 feet, or 1.8 m)

INSTRUCTIONS

1. Cut a length of embroidery floss that is about 8 feet (2.4 m) long.

2. Tie a large, secure knot 1 foot (30 cm) from one end of the floss. If you have wooden beads, tie one into the knot to prevent any flowers from slipping off the end.

3. Thread your needle onto the other end of the floss. Slide the needle almost to the middle of your string to make it easier to work with.

4. Choose a flower head to begin your flower bunting. With the needle, pierce the top of the flower in the center, aiming the needle to emerge out of the stem on the bottom of the head. Gently slide the flower all the way to the knotted end of your string. If your flower slips off the knot, tie a larger knot or thread your first flower head sideways through the thick, green section below the petals.

5. If you are using the wooden beads, decide how frequently you will string them. If you will place one between each flower head, it's time to thread one.

6. Thread your next flower through the center and out the stem and gently slide it until it rests against the first flower.

7. Repeat this process until you have used all your blossoms. You will need to move your needle part way through to prevent losing the tail of your string inside the flower chain.

8. When you are satisfied with your flower bunting, tie a final substantial knot at the end of your flower string, knotting in a wooden bead (if using). Trim your tails to be roughly even, about 1 foot (30 cm) each.

9. Hang your bunting from a picnic shelter, from a low tree branch, or across a window frame or doorway. Beautiful!

TIP

Many flowers remain sturdy and colorful even after they dry. Bring your bunting indoors after your party and allow it to air-dry. You can use it to decorate your room all year!

RAIN PAINTING

Artist Andy Goldsworthy creates art using only his hands and body, things he finds in nature, and a pocketknife. His work is fanciful and usually temporary, which is certainly part of its magic. A week, a day, or a moment after the art is completed, the landscape returns to normal, unaffected by his time spent making art from leaves, grass, twigs, and stone. One quick and simple project that Andy's work inspired is to use your body to create a stencil, leaving a fleeting impression of yourself during a rainfall.

SUPPLIES

* ✳ Dry pavement or sand in an area that cars and bikes do not use
* ✳ An impending rainstorm
* ✳ Your body!

TIME: under 5 minutes
YIELD: 1 rain painting

INSTRUCTIONS

1. As the first drops of rain begin to fall, lay your body on the sun-warmed pavement or in the sand. Pose however you wish. The more dramatic the better!

2. Lie still while the rain soaks you thoroughly. When you feel drenched, your painting should be ready.

3. Stand up quickly and admire the outline of you that the rain has silhouetted on the pavement or sand.

4. Watch as it disappears in moments—then run for shelter!

LOCAL FOOD POTLUCK

Wherever you live, it's likely there is locally grown food nearby. In cities and towns, weekly farmers' markets are common during the growing season. Here, you can buy food directly from the farmer. Ask your local grocery store if they carry any local produce, meats, cheeses, or breads or join a community garden and grow your own! If you live in the country, keep an eye out for roadside farm stands.

   Then, celebrate this local abundance with a local food potluck! Challenge your guests to find at least one local ingredient to include in the dish they bring to the party. It could be herbs they grow in a pot on their patio, zucchini from a friend's garden, or local eggs and milk baked into a loaf of bread or some cookies.

SUPPLIES
* ❋ Party invitations
* ❋ Pencils or pens
* ❋ Index cards

INSTRUCTIONS

1. Send your friends and family invitations to your potluck. Let them know the date, time, and location.

2. In your invitation, tell them the party is a potluck, where each guest brings a dish to share. Encourage them to bring a dish cooked with one or more local ingredients and request they bring a few copies of their recipe to share.

3. Ask your guests to bring reusable picnic plates, cups, silverware, napkins, and a picnic blanket or camping chair, if desired.

4. On the day of the party, set up your potluck area before your guests arrive. Set out any picnic blankets you may have and dress a picnic table with an outdoor tablecloth. Have a few sets of picnic dishes on hand in case anyone forgot their own.

5. Set out index cards and pencils or pens with a sign on the table instructing your guests to label their food by writing the name of their dish on an index card, including the local ingredients they used and who grew the ingredient (if they know)! They can place copies of the recipes beside their dish so interested partygoers can snap up a copy to take home.

BARK-AND-LEAF BOAT REGATTA

The simple pleasure of crafting miniature boats from scraps of wood, twigs, and leaves is a summer highlight. The first time my children and I made leaf boats, we were out until bedtime building and launching boats as the sun slipped behind the hills.

Use whatever scraps you can find to build your boats. Some will float; others with flop. I think that's part of the fun. Anchors aweigh!

SUPPLIES

* ❋ Water location to float your boats (stream, pond, pool, tub, etc.)
* ❋ Bits of tree bark, driftwood, or lumber scraps for hulls
* ❋ Fallen sticks or sturdy green stems, for masts
* ❋ Fresh, sturdy leaves (pictured are maple, mullein, violet, and oak), for sails
* ❋ Pocketknife or awl (optional)

TIME: under 20 minutes per boat

INSTRUCTIONS

1. Gather your supplies close to the location where you plan to float your boats. Begin by floating your boat hull (scrap of lumber or tree bark) to determine which side should be up.

2. Carve out a small hole in the hull for your mast and then fit a twig into the hole. Add a leaf sail, if you'd like, and other details as inspiration strikes. (My kids sometimes add flowers or flower petals, acorns, pebbles, or other cargo and decorations.)

3. Set sail! Launch your boat into the water from the shore or a dock. Adjust as needed and watch as your craft sails away into the sunset—or sinks to the bottom of the pond!

GIANT BUBBLES

Ready to blow some bubbles that will blow your mind? These homemade bubble wands and bubble solution make for the biggest bubbles I have ever seen. And they couldn't be easier to make. No special materials are required—just a couple sticks and some string and you're on your way to the biggest bubbles ever.

The recipe for the bubble solution by Jackie Currie from Happy Hooligans, which she kindly let me share with you, has been my family's go-to since the first time we tried it. It's the best there is!

BUBBLE WAND SUPPLIES

* Two 12- to 18-inch (30 to 46 cm) sticks, about the diameter of your thumb
* Pocketknife or branch cutter
* Drill with a drill bit slightly narrower than the diameter of your screw eyes (optional)
* Two ¼-inch (6 mm) screw eyes
* One 6-foot (1.8 m)-long piece cotton yarn or kitchen string
* 1 small metal nut or washer (½- to ¾-inch, or 1 to 2 cm, diameter)

BUBBLE SOLUTION INGREDIENTS

* Suitably sized pail
* 6 cups (1.4 L) warm water
* ½ cup (64 g) cornstarch
* ½ cup (120 ml) heavy-duty dish soap (See Note at bottom.)
* 1 tablespoon (5 g) baking powder
* 1 tablespoon (15 ml) glycerin

TIME: under 20 minutes

YIELD: 1 bubble wand, 6 cups (1.4 L) bubble solution

INSTRUCTIONS

PART 1: MAKE YOUR BUBBLE WAND

1. Trim your sticks to remove any side branches. Drill a hole in one end of each branch for your screw eyes.

2. Twist the screw eyes into your pilot holes until they are snug.

3. Thread your cotton string through the screw eyes. Slip the washer onto the string and then secure with an overhand knot.

(continued)

NOTE

This project is very adaptable to whatever materials you have on hand! Use dowels instead of branches or search your toolbox for screw eyes and washers of any size or description.

I have tried making bubbles with natural dish soap but found the bubbles were not strong enough to release from the string. The bubbles pictured were created with blue Dawn dish soap, but any heavy-duty dish soap should work.

PART 2: MAKE YOUR BUBBLE SOLUTION

1. In your pail, stir together the water and cornstarch, stirring well to dissolve the cornstarch.

2. Gently stir in the dish soap, baking powder, and glycerin, being careful not to create a lot of froth on the surface of your bubble solution.

PART 3: BLOW GIANT BUBBLES

It's time to blow bubbles! Here's how:

1. Pick up your bubble wand sticks with the screw eyes and string facing away from you.

2. Hold the screw eyes close together and completely submerge the yarn in the bubble solution. (If your yarn is dry it will float the first time you try to submerge it. Keep at it until it sinks.)

3. Lift the wand carefully from the juice and slowly separate the sticks to open the yarn loop.

4. Walk slowly backward into the wind and watch your bubbles soar!

5. You can encourage smaller (though still huge!) bubbles to break off and fly free by bringing the yarn loop back together to snip off a bubble here and there.

TIP

If your bubble solution gets frothy on the top from use, give it a few minutes to settle down. It works best without foam. Only dip one wand in the solution at a time to prevent the strings from becoming tangled.

DARK AND LIGHT IN BALANCE ONCE MORE

From the Summer Solstice until the Autumn Equinox, days grow gradually shorter until night and day are in balance again. On the day of the Autumn Equinox, dark and light exist in equal parts, about twelve hours of each per day. Only twice each year do day and night briefly come into balance—at the turning points of the year in spring and autumn. The word "equinox" means just this, equal night and day.

AUTUMN

AUTUMN EQUINOX: PREPARING FOR WINTER

➤→ **September 23** in the Northern Hemisphere

➤→ **March 21** in the Southern Hemisphere

As summer slowly fades into autumn, plants and animals make their final rush of preparations before winter comes. Autumn is the time when many plants become dormant and animals either leave on migration or settle in for colder, darker days.

Around our human homes, we busily stack firewood, harvest crops, and air out our wool sweaters and winter boots for the coming cold weather. Fall means back to school and the quiet shift from the outward energy of summer to the inward stillness and rest of the coming colder days.

A SEASON OF REST

Triggered by the shorter, cooler days, deciduous trees begin to draw the last of their energy from their leaves, storing it deep in their roots. As the leaves shut down, their green color fades, revealing a brilliant rainbow of color hidden from sight all summer long. Yellows, oranges, browns, purples, and reds all brighten the autumn landscape before the leaves, one by one, drop to the ground to feed the tree in the year that follows.

Also triggered by the shortening days, animals complete their preparations for winter—leaving on their long migration to warmer equatorial regions, preparing for hibernation, or stockpiling food for the lean season to come. Autumn carries its own abundance, helping animals with a last fill-up on nourishing, high-fat foods like nuts and seeds, as well as fruits to fuel them for the months to come.

MULLED CIDER

Just over the hill from my house is a small organic apple orchard. My family loves to pick apples there each autumn for eating fresh and making applesauce and apple butter. And, I can never resist picking up a jug or two of fresh apple cider. What's my favorite way to drink it? Slowly mulled with warming autumn spices and sipped from a favorite mug beside a crackling fire.

Don't feel limited if you're out of one or more of the spices listed. Like most recipes, this one is quite forgiving, so add or subtract spices as you wish. If you'd like to experiment with other combinations, try adding a twist of lemon zest, several orange slices, a pinch of nutmeg, or a few whole peppercorns.

INGREDIENTS

* ✳ 1 quart (946 ml) organic apple cider
* ✳ 1-inch (2.5 cm) piece fresh ginger, peeled and sliced
* ✳ 6 green cardamom pods or 2 teaspoons cardamom seeds
* ✳ Whole cinnamon sticks (1 per serving)
* ✳ 2 star anise pods
* ✳ 1 teaspoon whole cloves
* ✳ ½ teaspoon whole allspice berries

TIME: under 40 minutes, or up to 4 hours with a longer steeping time

YIELD: 1 quart (946 ml)

INSTRUCTIONS

1. In a large cooking pot, combine the apple cider and spices.

2. Place the pot over medium heat and cook until the liquid is just below a simmer. Reduce the heat to low.

3. Cover the pot and warm gently, stirring occasionally, for a minimum of 30 minutes or up to 4 hours.

4. Serve warm, with a cinnamon stick as a straw, if desired.

SPICED HONEY

❖─────────────────❖

When I was young my dad was a beekeeper, keeping a few beehives buzzing happily away in a corner of our backyard. I still remember the first time I looked into a bucket of just-extracted honey, marveling at the magic the honeybees created, right there in my own backyard.

This recipe is one of the few ways I know to improve on the bee's own perfection. Add some warm autumn spices to your honey jar and infuse even more flavor into every precious drop.

INGREDIENTS

* ✳ 12 cardamom pods or 1 teaspoon whole cardamom seeds
* ✳ 12 whole cloves
* ✳ 9 whole allspice berries
* ✳ 3 star anise pods
* ✳ 2-inch (5 cm) piece fresh ginger, peeled and thinly sliced
* ✳ 2 whole cinnamon sticks
* ✳ 1½ cups (510 g) honey, at room temperature

ACTIVE TIME: under 15 minutes

TOTAL TIME: 2 days to 1 week

YIELD: about 1½ cups (510 g)

INSTRUCTIONS

1. In a clean, dry pint-size (473 ml) jar, combine all of the spices.

2. Pour the honey over the spices. Use a kitchen knife or chopstick to help the honey fill the air spaces and surround the spices.

3. Continue gently poking at the spices with the knife or chopstick until all air bubbles are removed.

4. Tightly cover your jar; label the lid with the date and contents.

5. Fill a large cooking pot halfway with warm water, about the temperature of bath water.

6. Place your jar in the pot of hot water, being careful not to submerge the jar above the lid. This added warmth will help the honey liquefy, if crystalized, and encourage the infusion along.

7. Let infuse for 2 hours or more, removing the honey and reheating the water until just warm anytime you notice it has gone cold.

8. Repeat this process at least once a day (more often if you think of it), for a minimum of 2 days or up to 1 week. Taste daily until you are pleased with the flavor.

9. Gently warm in a hot water bath one final time.

10. Remove the lid and pour the honey through a fine-mesh strainer set over a clean, dry measuring pitcher. Use a rubber spatula to scrape as much precious honey as you can from your infusing jar. (Do not wash the jar; set it aside.)

11. Allow the honey to strain from the spices for at least 15 minutes and then return the spices from the strainer to the infusing jar.

12. Transfer your strained honey to a half-pint (235 ml) jar. Cover, label, and date the jar.

13. To get the most out of the honey left on the sides of your jar and still coating your spices, fill the jar with gently warmed water. Stir well and let infuse for 30 minutes and then strain, cover the jar, and refrigerate. Use this spicy sweet infused water for cooking oatmeal or add a splash to freshly brewed tea. Use or discard within 6 days.

TO USE

Add your spiced honey to tea, warm milk, applesauce, or cooked cereal—anywhere you'd enjoy a little warm, spicy sweetness. Stored in a cool, dark cupboard, infused honey will keep for 1 year.

NATURE NOTES

Did you know that in its lifetime a honeybee produces about 1 teaspoon of honey? This fact makes me want to savor every spoonful.

HOMEMADE APPLESAUCE

Whether you pick your apples off a backyard tree or pick them up at the grocery store, fresh autumn apples beg to be cooked into applesauce. Choose crisp, tart apples for the finest flavor.

INGREDIENTS

- ✳ 1 tablespoon (15 ml) fresh lemon juice
- ✳ 6¾ cups (1.6 L) water, divided
- ✳ 6 tart, medium-size apples (about 2 pounds or 900 g)
- ✳ 1 teaspoon ground cinnamon
- ✳ 2 to 4 tablespoons (40 to 80 g) honey or maple syrup (optional)

TIME: under 30 minutes

YIELD: 1 generous pint (about 473 ml)

INSTRUCTIONS

1. In a large bowl, combine the lemon juice and 6 cups (1.4 L) of water.

2. One at a time, wash, peel, and core your apples, slipping each into your lemon juice bath when finished (to prevent browning).

3. One at a time, remove the apples from the lemon juice bath and roughly chop each apple into 1-inch (2.5 cm) cubes, returning the pieces to the lemon juice bath.

4. When all the apples are peeled and chopped, use a large slotted spoon to transfer them to a medium-size cooking pot.

5. Add the remaining ¾ cup (175 ml) of water and place the pot, uncovered, over medium heat. Cook until the water beneath the apples begins to simmer.

6. Carefully stir in the cinnamon. Cover the pot and turn the heat to low.

7. Cook for 15 to 20 minutes, stirring the apples every few minutes using a sturdy, long-handled spoon. Add more water ¼ cup (60 ml) at a time, as needed, if the water in the bottom of the pot has evaporated.

8. When the apples become quite soft and begin to break down, your sauce is nearly ready! Remove it from the heat. Cool a spoonful of your sauce and taste it, adding honey or maple syrup as desired to sweeten the sauce. Enjoy warm or cold.

9. Refrigerate leftovers in an airtight container and enjoy within 10 days or freeze for up to 3 months.

PLANTING BULBS

Tucking flower bulbs into the ground in autumn creates a magical display come springtime! Tulips, daffodils, crocuses, and even the exotic-looking checkered fritillaria are all a cinch to plant and require very little care once established. The best part is, the effort of planting is long forgotten when the first spring flowers begin to appear!

SUPPLIES

* ❋ Assorted fall bulbs
* ❋ Trowel
* ❋ Compost (1 trowelful per bulb; optional)
* ❋ Filled watering can

TIME: under 30 minutes

INSTRUCTIONS

1. Choose a sunny, dry place to plant your bulbs. Avoid areas that are in deep shade or frequently muddy. Choose an out-of-the-way location where they won't be trampled by pets or people.

2. Dig down 4 to 8 inches (10 to 20 cm), loosening the soil and removing rocks and roots. (Planting depth varies by species, so follow any planting instructions that came with your bulbs or follow the rule of thumb to plant any bulb twice as deep as the bulb is tall.)

3. If using, add a scoop of compost to each hole before planting your bulbs.

4. Place your bulbs at the proper depth, with the wider, rougher root end facing down and the narrower, pointed end facing up.

5. Cover with soil and gently tamp it down.

6. If using, add another scoop of compost on top to provide needed nutrients to the bulbs.

7. Water well on planting day and then leave your bulbs to rest until spring. When your flowers push up and bloom, harvest as many as you'd like or leave them in the garden for a lasting show. When the flowers die back, don't immediately cut away the leaves, as they feed the roots and promote blooms for years to come.

TIP

Plant bulbs when daytime temperatures are consistently between 40°F and 50°F (4.4°C to 10°C), normally in early to mid-autumn. In climates that experience freezing winter temperatures, plant your bulbs 1½ to 2 months before the ground freezes for best results. (If you live in a warmer climate, bulbs can be planted at the very end of fall, as late as December in the Northern Hemisphere and June in the Southern.)

NOTE

If you don't have a yard of your own, ask a friend or neighbor if you can plant bulbs at their house to enjoy in the springtime. When the flowers bloom, you both can share the blossoms for bouquets in your homes.

NATURE NOTES

Did you know? A single bulb can become a whole bouquet, given enough time and patience. Bulbs like tulips, crocuses, and daffodils often spread, resulting in more blooms with each passing year. Expect one flower per bulb the first year, but some will double (then triple, then possibly even more) beginning with year two.

CREATE AN AUTUMN RAINBOW

The art we create needn't last forever! This temporary installation requires only a handful of colorful leaves, a not-too-windy day, and your imagination. (And, it's even more fun to make with friends.)

TIME: under 10 minutes to assemble, plus time to collect fall leaves

YIELD: 1 leaf art piece

INSTRUCTIONS

1. On a sunny, low-wind, autumn day, head out around your neighborhood to collect colorful fallen leaves. Bring along a basket or cloth shopping bag to store them in while you walk.

2. Back home or at your neighborhood park, find a flat piece of ground to serve as your canvas, clearing away sticks and stray leaves.

3. Arrange your leaves by color near your Earth canvas and then begin to assemble a rainbow from the leaves you have collected. Experiment with other shapes, like a sunburst, spiral, or any other pattern you're inspired to lay out on the ground.

4. Stand back and admire your work! If you're still feeling artistic, make another with any leaves you still have in your basket.

FELTED ACORN NECKLACES

Felted acorns are sweet, simple, and fun to make. Using the instructions here, make a bowlful for play or attach a string to each to make a necklace. Use whatever colors of wool you can find. (Because who said acorns can't be purple?)

SUPPLIES

* Absorbent towels
* Two medium-size bowls or cooking pots with stable bases
* Hot and cold water
* Dish soap
* Wool roving (see the Resources section, page 137, for where to buy), about 3 inches (7.5 cm) length per acorn
* Acorn cap
* Drill and small drill bit (about 3/32 inch or 2.5 mm)
* Hand sewing needle that will fit your thread
* 24 inches (60 cm) of thin hemp cord or embroidery floss, in color of your choice
* Tacky glue or hot glue

TIME: under 15 minutes per acorn, plus drying time

YIELD: 1 felted acorn

INSTRUCTIONS

1. Cover your work surface with absorbent towels.

2. Half-fill one bowl with the hottest water you can comfortably dip your hands into. Add a squirt of dish soap and stir to combine.

3. Half-fill another bowl with cold water and place the two bowls side by side on your covered work surface.

4. Gently tear off a 3-inch (7.5 cm) length of wool roving and tease it apart into loose, parallel strands. Once teased apart, it should cover your palm and fingers with a light, fluffy layer of wool you can see your hand through.

5. Tear the wool into four roughly equal lengths. Stack three of them, alternating the direction of the fibers. (Lay the first layer with the fibers running left to right; the second with fibers running up and down; and the third with fibers running left to right again.) Set the fourth section aside.

6. Gently roll this stack of wool into a very loose, messy ball in your hand. Continue rolling until it is about the size of a small lime or clementine.

TIP

Felting wool takes time. At first, it will seem like it isn't working! Be patient and you'll be rewarded with the cutest little woolen acorns ever.

(continued)

7. Dip the ball into the hot, soapy water, lift out, and squeeze. It will become flat and floppy, but don't despair!

8. Using a very light touch, gently roll the wet wool into a ball shape once more. Note: If you try to make a tight ball right away by applying too much pressure, the wool will remain flat and refuse to cooperate. Apply the smallest amount of pressure at first, gradually increasing it as the ball begins to take shape and become firm.

9. After your (still messy) ball begins to take shape and become more solid, dip your wool into the cold water, remove it, and squeeze. Roll the wool briefly between your hands, dip it into the hot water bath once more, and squeeze and roll again.

10. Repeat this process, gradually adding more and more pressure, until a firm ball takes shape. At first, it will be quite messy with folds and fissures, but as you work, these imperfections will fade.

11. Once your ball is roughly the size of an overgrown acorn, tease apart your reserved section of wool and wrap it gently around the ball to cover any deep cracks. Dip the ball into the hot water and continue working as before (as described in step 8).

12. When you are pleased with your work, roll your woolen ball into a slightly oblong shape that will fit into your acorn cap. Test the fit and adjust the ball as needed to create a pleasing shape.

13. Squeeze out excess water and let air-dry.

14. Meanwhile, prepare your acorn cap. Drill two holes in the top, on opposite sides of the stem. Thread your needle with embroidery floss. Pass the needle through the cap beginning with the needle going up from the underside in one hole and then sending it back down through the other. Knot off with an overhand knot.

15. Pull the thread up from the cap, centering the knot inside the acorn cap, where it will be concealed by the acorn.

16. When your woolen acorn is thoroughly dry, add a dab of glue to the inside of your acorn cap and insert the wool acorn. Hold the cap firmly in place until the glue is dry.

TIP

If you don't have access to wool roving, you can still craft your own acorns using scrap fabric from discarded clothing. Cut a 2-inch (5 cm) circle out of an old T-shirt, leggings, or a thin sweater. Place a cotton ball inside for stuffing and then gather the edges of the bundle together like a parcel, forming your acorn. Secure the raw edges with a few stitches, knot to secure, and trim away excess fabric. Tuck the sewn end of your acorn into your cap to check the fit and then proceed with steps 14 through 16.

Light tufts of wool become dense wool felt when treated to temperature fluctuations (hot-cold-hot-cold) and friction (rubbing the fibers between our hands). Keep applying friction and changing the temperature of the wool and (with a little time and patience) you'll begin to see results!

WAXED LEAF GARLAND

A string of waxed leaves looks delightful hanging across a doorway or above your kitchen table. Carefully stored, the leaves will last for years without losing their brilliant fall colors.

SUPPLIES

- ✽ 20 to 30 colorful, freshly fallen leaves
- ✽ 2 pounds (900 g) beeswax (see the Resources section, page 137, for where to buy)
- ✽ Medium-size cooking pot, double-boiler, or electric slow cooker (reserved for wax use only), large enough to accommodate your leaves
- ✽ Newspaper or utility cloths
- ✽ Waxed paper
- ✽ Clean stick (stripped of bark) or a wooden skewer
- ✽ 12 feet (3.6 m) thin hemp cord, cotton kitchen string, or embroidery floss

TIME: under 1½ hours, not including leaf collecting

YIELD: one 8-foot (2.4 m) garland

INSTRUCTIONS

STEP 1: WAX YOUR LEAVES

1. Gather your leaves on a rain-free day, after the morning dew has dried. Collect your leaves in a basket or sturdy bag to prevent crumpling or tearing. Bring your leaves indoors.

2. Place the beeswax in your slow cooker, cover the cooker, and slowly melt on medium or low heat. Alternatively, place the wax in a medium-size pot and place the pot over medium-low heat on the stovetop to melt the wax. Watch it closely, as the wax can burn if it becomes too hot.

3. While the wax melts, set up your work area. Cover your floor and work surface with newspaper or utility cloths and lay out a 2-foot (60 cm)-long piece of waxed paper.

4. When the wax has fully melted, turn off the heat.

5. Hold one leaf by the stem and dip it into the wax. If needed, push the leaf under the surface of the wax using your wooden skewer or stick.

6. Carefully lift the leaf out of the wax and hold it for a moment over the pot to allow drips to fall back in, and to allow the leaf to cool and the wax to set.

7. Carefully transfer the coated leaf to the waxed paper to cool completely.

8. Repeat with additional leaves, reheating your pot of wax as needed if it begins to set.

STEP 2: MAKE YOUR GARLAND

1. When your leaves are fully cooled, it's time to make your garland! Choose your largest or most beautiful leaf and set it aside.

2. Tie a loose knot in the center of your string, leaving an opening the size of your fingertip in the center of the knot. Insert the stem of your chosen leaf into this opening and then gently pull the string to secure the stem.

3. About 1 to 2 inches (2.5 to 5 cm) from your center leaf in either direction, repeat this process with a second leaf. Continue tying leaves to your string until you have a 2-foot (60 cm) tail remaining on each side or when you run out of waxed leaves.

4. Display your garland by hanging across a doorway, above your dining table, or anywhere you want to add a bit of autumn beauty.

NOTE

You'll need a designated double boiler or slow cooker for this project—one that will be reserved for beeswax going forward. Pick one up at a garage sale or secondhand store rather than buying it new. Avoid pots lined with Teflon or other nonstick coatings, which may scrape off into your wax. When your project is finished, let the wax cool in the pot, cover it, and store until your next project.

GRATITUDE TREE

Gratitude and harvest festivals are enjoyed around the world, from Vietnam to India, Germany to Ghana. Every autumn, my own family gathers to celebrate all we are grateful for. At the center of our celebration table is a simple tree branch bearing an assortment of paper leaves, each one noting something that one of us appreciates. It has become a favorite family tradition—one that reminds us of all we have to be grateful for.

SUPPLIES

- ✳ Branch cutter
- ✳ Sturdy tree branch, about 3 feet (90 cm) tall
- ✳ Stable vase or large Mason jar
- ✳ Marbles or small stones to stabilize vase (optional)
- ✳ Paper in autumn colors
- ✳ Small hole punch (optional)
- ✳ Large metal darning needle
- ✳ Yarn or string that will fit through your needle
- ✳ Scissors
- ✳ Pencils
- ✳ Basket or bowl

TIME: under 30 minutes to assemble plus time to write and read blessings

YIELD: 1 gratitude tree

INSTRUCTIONS

PART 1: PREPARE YOUR TREE AND LEAVES

1. Head outside to choose a sturdy, not-too-big branch to place on your table.

2. Using your branch cutters, trim any long or awkward twigs to help it fit more comfortably on your table.

3. If desired, carefully fill your vase with marbles or stones. This will help prevent tipping if the branch is bumped. To fill your vase, lay it on its side and gently roll the marbles or stones inside and then slowly stand the jar upright after all the marbles are added. Do not drop the stones into the upright jar, as it can break the glass.

4. Cut simple leaf shapes out of colored paper.

5. Using your hole punch or darning needle, make a hole near the stem end of each leaf.

6. Thread your darning needle with yarn and run a 5-inch (13 cm) length of yarn through the hole in each leaf. Secure with an overhand knot.

PART 2: SHARE YOUR GRATITUDE

1. Place your branch or bowl in the center of your table. Scatter the paper leaves around the vase and set out enough pencils for each family member or guest.

2. Throughout the day, instruct your family or guests to write or draw anything they feel grateful for onto the leaves.

3. When the leaves are used up and everyone has contributed one or more things they are grateful for, place the leaves in a basket for sharing.

4. Pass the basket, instructing everyone to choose a few to read. Non-readers can share illustrated leaves or help a sibling or adult share their leaves.

5. Take turns reading aloud and sharing the things your family is grateful for.

NOTE

If you don't have easy access to a tree branch where you live, or have very young children in your home, skip the branch and simply place a large, wide bowl on the table to drop the leaves into instead. It's still a beautiful display and is more toddler friendly than the branch. (If you will be using a bowl, skip all but number 4 in step 1 of the instructions.)

TIP

If your guests experience "writer's block," let them know anything goes! From the everyday comforts we often take for granted (our home, a cozy bed, running water, food in the pantry), special rare treats (a visit from Grandma, ice cream sundaes, or an upcoming trip), or any of the countless things we treasure about one another—they're all things to be grateful for.

BOUNTIFUL HARVEST EXCHANGE

Gather with friends and family to celebrate the abundance of harvest season. Share your garden or kitchen bounty and then bring home a few treats to enjoy from your friends' harvests as well.

Enjoy any or all of the autumn festivities following or create your own celebration with the recipes and projects found in this chapter.

HOLIDAY: Autumn Equinox

LOCATION: Gather with friends and family in your own backyard or in a neighborhood park. If possible, choose a location where you can have a small campfire. In the weather is uncooperative, move the party to a picnic shelter or indoors to a community room at your local library or your own kitchen or dining room. Adapt activities and snacks as needed.

DECORATIONS: Pumpkins, Decorative Lanterns (page 92), and a campfire (if permitted)

FOOD AND DRINK: Mulled Cider (page 75), Bonfire Bread (page 95), and Baked Apples (page 98)

ACTIVITIES: Gratitude Tree (page 88), Autumn Rainbow (page 82), and Autumn Abundance Exchange (page 100)

PARTY FAVORS: Felted Acorn Necklaces (page 83) or Decorative Lanterns (page 92)

DECORATIVE LANTERNS AND CANDLE-LIT LANTERN WALK

As fall moves slowly toward winter, the nights become longer and the days grow short and dark. A lantern walk, enjoyed in late autumn, is a wonderful way to bring light to the darkness, while celebrating the changing season with family and friends.

DECORATIVE LANTERN SUPPLIES

* Drop cloths or newsprint
* Upcycled, sturdy glass jar (half-pint, pint-, or quart-size, or 235, 473, or 946 ml jars work well)
* Colorful translucent paper, kite paper works best (see the Resources section, page 137, for where to buy), or use colored tissue paper
* Scissors
* Mod Podge craft glue or diluted white glue (2 parts glue to 1 part water)
* Small disposable bowl for the glue (the lid from one of your jars would be perfect)
* ½ to 1-inch (1 to 2.5 cm)-wide craft paintbrush
* Wire cutters
* Needle-nose pliers
* Flexible wire

LANTERN WALK SUPPLIES

* 1 lantern per person
* Sturdy forked sticks to hold the lanterns (optional)
* Candles or battery-powered candles
* Poster putty or double-sided craft adhesive (optional)
* Matches

TIME: under 1 hour, plus drying time and 30 minutes for the walk

INSTRUCTIONS

PART 1: MAKE YOUR LANTERN

1. Cover your table with a drop cloth or a few layers of newsprint.

2. If necessary, remove the label and any adhesive from your jars (lavender or sweet orange essential oil work well for this). Let the jars dry.

3. Prepare your kite paper: Cut it into simple shapes like stars, circles, and triangles or tear or cut your paper into ½ to 1½-inch (1 to 3.8 cm) strips.

4. Pour a bit of Mod Podge into your bowl and using your paintbrush, coat the outside of the jar with a thin layer of Mod Podge.

5. Place overlapping kite paper shapes onto your jar, pressing gently to adhere. Use your brush (dipped in Mod Podge) to smooth the paper and reduce wrinkles.

6. Continue placing shapes all around your jar. Let dry.

7. After the Mod Podge has dried, add a second layer to the outside to seal and protect the paper.

8. There is no right or wrong way to attach your wire handle, as long as your method creates a 10-inch (25 cm) or longer wire loop to carry from and is secure. I have outlined my favorite method here, if you're looking for a bit more guidance.

9. Cut one 18 to 24-inch (46 to 60 cm) length of wire. Using a pair of pliers, bend a hook on one end of your wire. Wrap this end of the wire around the jar neck until it makes a complete circle, overlapping another section of your wire loop. Pass the hook over the overlapping wire and pinch closed with pliers to secure.

10. Bend a 90-degree angle into your wire just above the point where the hook has been secured. Using your pliers, create another hook at the remaining unattached end of your wire. Bring the long wire tail up and over the neck of your jar and secure on the opposite side of the jar by pinching the second hook closed.

11. Tighten the wire around the neck, if needed, by bending several S curves into the wire that encircles the jar neck.

(continued)

PART 2: TAKE A LANTERN WALK

Enjoy a peaceful lantern walk with your family on a dark, autumn night. What a magical way to celebrate the turning of the year!

1. Around sunset, gather with friends or family for a quiet, candle-lit walk around your neighborhood or a local park. If you have access to a safe place that lacks streetlights, all the better. (Though even under streetlights, the lanterns are a beautiful sight.)

2. Place a candle in the bottom of each lantern, securing it with poster putty or double-sided craft adhesive, if desired, to prevent slipping. Carefully light the candles.

3. Suspend each lantern from a sturdy, forked stick (if desired), holding the stick at an upward angle to prevent the lantern from falling. Or, carry your lantern by hand, using the attached wire loop as a handle.

4. Gather in a circle to take in the beauty of the lanterns as they light the darkness. Then, set off on a peaceful walk around the block or the park.

5. When you return to your starting point, circle up once more before extinguishing your lights and returning home.

INDOOR ALTERNATIVE

If you prefer to celebrate indoors, omit the handles on your lanterns and arrange them safely in your home. Turn off the electric lights and quietly gather with family or friends for a candle-lit evening indoors.

SAFETY PRECAUTIONS

Setting a calm, peaceful tone for your candle-lit walk is a must. Walking slowly and being respectful of one another is required of all who participate. The children I have taken on candle-lit walks love the responsibility of carefully transporting a candle in the darkness, but if you feel your family would do best with electronic candles, use them instead. If using real candles, teach the children on your walk how to hold the candle carefully, away from hair, clothing, and other participants. Young children can help an adult, carrying one lantern together.

BONFIRE BREAD

Tasty treats cooked outside on a fall day are autumn perfection. This bonfire bread (also known as Danish *snobrød*) is as much fun to make as it is to eat. If you're making the dough for your party and need extra time, make it the night before, but let it rise overnight in the refrigerator (instead of on the counter for 1 hour).

BONFIRE BREAD INGREDIENTS

* ✳ 2 tablespoons (28 g) unsalted butter, plus more for serving (optional)
* ✳ 1 cup (235 ml) warm water
* ✳ 2 teaspoons sugar or honey
* ✳ 1½ teaspoons salt
* ✳ 1 tablespoon plus 1½ teaspoons (18 g) instant yeast or 2 packets
* ✳ 3 cups (375 g) all-purpose flour or 2 cups (250 g) all-purpose flour plus 1 cup (120 g) whole-wheat flour, divided
* ✳ Jam, for serving (optional)

ACTIVE TIME: under 45 minutes

TOTAL TIME: under 1½ hours (not including time to make the campfire and prepare the coals)

YIELD: serves 8

BONFIRE SUPPLIES

* ✳ Campfire circle or pit
* ✳ Larger, dry hardwood firewood
* ✳ Newspaper (black-and-white sheets only) or shredded birch bark
* ✳ Small, dry twigs or other kindling
* ✳ Matches
* ✳ Small pocket knife

(continued)

INSTRUCTIONS

PART 1: MAKE YOUR BREAD DOUGH

1. In a small saucepan over medium heat, warm the butter until just melted. Remove from the heat.

2. In a medium-size bowl, stir together the warm water, melted butter, sugar, and salt to combine. Test the temperature of your mixture, making sure it's just slightly warmer than body temperature (warm to the touch but not hot). Hot water will kill the yeast, preventing the bread from rising. If it's too hot, let cool for a few minutes before proceeding with step 3.

3. Sprinkle the yeast on top of the water mixture and gently stir to dissolve. Let rest for 5 minutes.

4. Set aside ¼ cup (31 g) of flour.

5. Add the remaining flour, ½ cup (63 g) at a time, to your yeast mixture and using a sturdy spoon, stir well to combine after each addition. Continue adding flour until the dough pulls together into a shaggy ball. Using your hands, work all but the reserved ¼ cup (31 g) of flour into the dough.

6. Sprinkle the reserved ¼ cup (31 g) of flour onto a kitchen work surface and transfer the dough to the floured surface. Knead the dough for 5 to 10 minutes until the dough becomes smooth.

7. Form the dough into a ball, return it to your mixing bowl, and cover with a clean, damp kitchen towel. Let rise for 1 hour or until the dough doubles in size. Place your bread in a portable, sealable storage container to make it easy to carry with you to the bonfire.

PART 2: BUILD YOUR CAMPFIRE

1. While the dough rises, prepare your campfire. In a safe fire ring or campfire pit, layer (from the bottom up): dry firewood, a ball of crumpled newsprint or a few medium strips of birch bark, tiny dry twigs, and medium (finger-size) dry twigs.

2. Light your fire by placing a match under the bark or newsprint.

3. After the paper or bark is lit and the small twigs begin to burn, gradually add larger and larger kindling until your fire is ready to receive small dry pieces of firewood without smothering it.

4. Add a few large pieces of dry hardwood and allow them to burn until a bed of coals begins to form. Note: Hardwood firewood makes for better cooking coals than softwoods like pine. Choose harder species, if possible, for your fire.

PART 3: BAKE YOUR BREAD

We'll bake our bread by twisting strips of dough around green tree branches and then baking them over the hot coals.

1. Harvest a few sturdy green tree branches to use to bake your bread (3 feet, or 90 cm, long is a good size to keep hands away from the fire). Using a pocketknife, strip about 5 inches (13 cm) of bark from the narrower end of each branch to prevent the bread from sticking to the wood.

2. Divide the bread dough into 8 small balls. Roll each ball into a rope about 1 foot (30 cm) long. Wrap the dough rope around the narrow end of your stick, pressing the ends into place to secure.

3. Hold the dough over the hot coals, rotating it slowly to prevent burning. Bake until the bread is crisp and a medium brown on the outside and cooked through, about 15 minutes.

4. Let the bread cool for a few minutes before enjoying plain or with butter and jam.

CAMPFIRE SAFETY

Campfires are a responsibility that requires our attention and respect. Always honor the campfire rules:

* Have a grown-up check local ordinances to be sure campfires are allowed in your region and at this time of year.

* Choose a campfire spot that is a minimum of 15 feet (4.5 m) from buildings, tents, trees, and shrubs. Never light a campfire beneath overhanging tree branches.

* Always use a safe campfire pit or stone fire circle. If you need to create a new fire pit, dig a hole 1 foot (30 cm) deep and encircle the hole with dry rocks.

* Clear your campfire area of leaves, tall grasses, and debris, creating a 10-foot (3 m) circle with your fire pit in the center.

* Never light a campfire on a windy day or during times of drought.

* Never leave a campfire unattended.

* When you are finished with your campfire, extinguish it completely. Thoroughly saturate it with water and then stir the coals with a stick. Saturate and stir again, ensuring that the coals are completely cold before walking away.

BAKED APPLES

The first time my family made these apples, my kids said they tasted like apple pie without the crust. I agree! Nothing tastes better when gathered around a fire on a crisp autumn day.

INGREDIENTS

* ❋ 3 tablespoons (weight varies) chopped nuts (Pecans, walnuts, and almonds are all delicious.)
* ❋ 3 tablespoons (42 g) unsalted butter, melted
* ❋ 1 tablespoon (20 g) maple syrup
* ❋ ¼ teaspoon ground cinnamon
* ❋ Generous pinch ground nutmeg
* ❋ Generous pinch ground ginger
* ❋ Generous pinch ground cloves
* ❋ Pinch salt
* ❋ 4 crisp, tart apples

ACTIVE TIME: under 20 minutes

TOTAL TIME: under 1 hour (plus time to prepare the campfire and coals)

YIELD: 4 baked apples

INSTRUCTIONS

1. In a small bowl, stir together the nuts, melted butter, maple syrup, cinnamon, nutmeg, ginger, ground cloves, and salt until well mixed. Set aside.

2. Core your apples by cutting the top off at an angle around the stem, similar to the way you would cut the top off a pumpkin. Trim the reserved tops flat and set aside.

3. Using a small metal spoon, scoop out the apple core to just below the seeds, leaving the bottom intact to create an apple cup to hold your filling. Compost or discard the core.

4. Fill each apple cup to just below the top with the filling. Place the reserved caps on top.

5. Individually wrap each apple in aluminum foil, twisting the foil at the top to seal. Alternately, the apples can be placed in a well-seasoned Dutch oven for baking.

6. Prepare your campfire (see Bonfire Bread, Build Your Campfire, page 96). Let the fire burn down to a bed of coals before baking your apples.

7. Using long heatproof tongs, carefully place the foil-wrapped apples onto the hot coals. Bake for 15 to 20 minutes, rotating them frequently. The apples are done when they yield to gentle pressure. Use the tongs to check for doneness to prevent burns.

8. Use your tongs to remove from the heat and let cool for 5 to 10 minutes before unwrapping. Scoop the soft, hot apple into a mug or small bowl and enjoy.

NO CAMPFIRE?

Bake your apples in the oven instead. Preheat the oven to 375°F (190°C, or gas mark 5). Prepare the apples following steps 1 and 2. Place the apples in an ovenproof casserole dish. Pour 1 to 2 cups (235 to 475 ml) water in the bottom of the pan (enough to cover the bottom of the pan by ½ to 1 inch, or 1 to 2.5 cm). Bake for 45 minutes or until soft.

AUTUMN ABUNDANCE EXCHANGE

As crops are harvested and gardens are put to bed, fall is a traditional time of year to gather with friends and celebrate the abundance of a successful growing season. Around the world, people gather with friends and family to share the bounty, expressing appreciation for friendship and food.

Why not start your own tradition? Even without a garden, we can still share the season's abundance by cooking, baking, or exchanging other handmade fall gifts, like Beeswax Candles (page 108) or Rose and Cardamom Herbal Tea (page 35). It's just another fine reason to get together with friends for food and fun!

SUPPLIES

* Party invitations
* An item you plan to exchange (see ideas following), 1 per party invitee

INSTRUCTIONS

1. Send your friends and family invitations to your Autumn Abundance Exchange. Tell them the date, time, location, and what to bring.

2. Let your guests know that your party is a harvest exchange, and each guest should bring six of one item from their kitchen, garden, or craft room to exchange for items brought by other friends (provide the list following for ideas). If desired, guests can also bring recipes or cards with other information about the items they are bringing to trade.

3. On the day of the party, set up a table where the harvest exchange will take place. Place a sign on the table that lets your guests know to lay out their items on the table and wait for further instructions.

4. When you are ready for the exchange to take place, gather with your guests around the table, taking turns choosing one item each they'd like to take home. After everyone has chosen their first item, cycle through again for a second. Repeat until everyone has six different items, trading if necessary with a friend to prevent duplicates or from bringing home your own item.

IDEAS OF ITEMS TO EXCHANGE

* Beeswax Candles (page 108)
* Breads, scones, crackers, muffins, or other home-baked goods
* Herbal First-Aid Balm (page 25)
* Homemade Applesauce (page 79)
* Homegrown, dried herbs
* Kitchen seasoning blends
* Pickles or other home-canned relishes
* Rose and Cardamom Herbal Tea (page 35), or other homemade herbal tea blends
* Sauerkraut
* Scented Play Dough (page 112)
* Sourdough starter
* Spiced Honey (page 76) or Rose Petal Honey (page 48)
* Winter squash, pumpkins, or other farmers' market bounty

THE LONGEST NIGHT

From the Autumn Equinox until the Winter Solstice, the days grow slowly shorter as the nights become longer. The hemisphere gradually cools, triggering leaves to fall, animals to migrate, and by the time winter arrives, many plants will have fallen into their own winter sleep.

On Winter Solstice, we experience the longest night of the year, while in the opposite hemisphere, they experience the longest day. This seasonal difference is caused by the tilt of the Earth (called "axial tilt"), which tips half of the planet away from the sun, and the other half toward it. Whatever is happening in one hemisphere (Northern or Southern) is the opposite of what is happening on the other side of the globe.

WINTER

WINTER SOLSTICE: LEAN DAYS OR A LONG REST

➥→ **December 21** in the Northern Hemisphere

➥→ **June 21** in the Southern Hemisphere

Winter is a long, deep pause. Its stillness offers a counterpoint to the hustle that rules the rest of the year and gives plants and animals—all of us—a chance to find our center again.

In winter, plants go dormant, and animals are either taking a long winter's rest, enduring the cold, or already off to warmer places on their fall migration. Even people are called hearthside to warm cold toes, sip tea, and watch the snow falling softly outside. There's no need to rush, and we too find ways to rest.

The long winter rest that some animals take, known as hibernation, is common for mammals, reptiles, and other animals in cold regions. Frogs, for example, bury themselves in the mud at the bottom of ponds, where their body systems slow to nearly a stop, and they quietly rest out the winter months.

Other animals, like many birds, remain active all winter long. They spend their days searching for high-energy food, and some spend their nights cuddled together with others of their species in a cozy mass of feathers and fluff. Still other species migrate in anticipation of the colder days, moving to warmer climates where food is more abundant during winter months.

Plants, too, take their own winter's rest, going dormant until longer, warmer days return at last.

WINTER STARGAZING

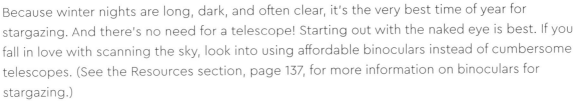

Because winter nights are long, dark, and often clear, it's the very best time of year for stargazing. And there's no need for a telescope! Starting out with the naked eye is best. If you fall in love with scanning the sky, look into using affordable binoculars instead of cumbersome telescopes. (See the Resources section, page 137, for more information on binoculars for stargazing.)

If you want a light to help you find your way, buy one that that won't impede your night vision or modify your flashlight to create a Night Vision Flashlight (page 111), which will not interfere with your eyes adjusting to the dark.

SUPPLIES

* Appropriate clothing for the weather
* A picnic blanket or other outdoor blanket for the ground (optional)
* A dark, ideally moonless, night
* An area free of direct light pollution (away from porches and streetlights and looking away from city lights, if possible)
* Night Vision Flashlight (page 111; optional)
* Star maps for your hemisphere (hand drawn from library books or other sources; optional)
* Thermos of hot tea or cocoa and mugs (optional)

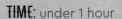

TIME: under 1 hour

INSTRUCTIONS

1. After dark, head outside to your viewing place and set it up by laying blankets on the ground, if desired.

2. Allow your eyes a chance to adjust to the darkness. It can take up to 40 minutes for your eyes to adjust fully, but even 10 minutes makes a big difference in what you can observe in the sky. No screens or flashlights are allowed while your eyes adjust. They will just set your night vision back to the start!

3. As your eyes adjust, begin searching the night sky for bright points of light. How many stars can you see?

4. Because of how our eyes work in low light, it's sometimes easier to see stars if we look just beside them instead of directly at them. As your eyes adjust, use this trick to be able to see the stars more clearly.

5. After your eyes have adjusted for 30 to 40 minutes, scan the sky again. Can you see more stars than you could before? That's your night vision working, adjusting your eyesight to the low light of the night.

6. While you stargaze, it's enjoyable to tell the same stories about constellations that our ancestors told one another hundreds, or even thousands, of years ago. Check the Resources section (page 137) for some ideas on where to find stories about the constellations you see above you, or if you're inspired, make up a few of your own!

PINECONE BIRD FEEDERS

Every season, I strive to do something helpful for the plants and animals in my neighborhood, to be a good caretaker of the Earth. From planting a tree each spring to picking up litter on summer hikes, it's easy to do small things to make the world a better place.

In winter, one of my favorite ways to care for nature is to feed the birds. I love putting together these simple pinecone and yarn bird feeders. The birds are crazy about the seed-studded peanut butter treats, and I love to watch their antics as they perch, spin, and feed outside my window.

SUPPLIES

* ❉ Outdoor tablecloth or drop cloth (optional, but nice to have)
* ❉ 2 cups (weight varies) birdseed of your choice
* ❉ Baking pan with tall sides (like a brownie pan or casserole dish)
* ❉ Scissors
* ❉ Kitchen string, twine, or yarn
* ❉ 4 medium to large pinecones or spruce cones
* ❉ Butter knives, one per person
* ❉ ½ cup (130 g) no-sugar-added peanut butter

TIME: under 30 minutes
YIELD: 4 bird feeders

INSTRUCTIONS

1. Ideally, set up your craft station in a carpet-free room that's easy to clean. If desired, spread the table with a washable tablecloth that you don't mind getting peanut buttery!

2. Pour the birdseed into a baking pan and set aside.

3. Cut a piece of string for each pinecone that is about 1 foot (30 cm) long. Wrap the center of the string around one end of the pinecone, working it through the scales toward the core.

4. Knot the string to secure it and then knot the two tails together to form a loop. Give your loop a very gentle tug to make sure it will hold. Repeat with the remaining pinecones.

5. Using your butter knife, spread peanut butter onto the pinecone, working it between the scales. Coat your pine cone completely, avoiding the loop of the string as best you can.

6. When you are satisfied with your coverage, pop your pinecone into the tray of birdseed.

7. This is a good time to pause your work to wash and dry your hands well. (This will keep you from becoming a bird feeder yourself, caked with seeds and peanut butter!) When your hands are thoroughly washed and dried, roll your pinecone around in the pan, pressing the seeds into the gaps between the cone scales. Keep rolling and pressing until you are satisfied with your seed coverage. There will be a few gaps; it doesn't have to be perfect.

8. Hang your bird feeder outside your window. (An area out of direct sunlight is ideal, but not necessary.) It may take a few days, or even a week, for the birds to find your feeders, but when they do, they'll be hungry to enjoy your generous offering.

BEESWAX CANDLES

Homemade candles give us more than just light. The experience of making them feels laced with old-time magic, and the scent of the melting wax is just heavenly. We give a bit of ourselves when we share these handmade gifts with our friends. Every year on the night of Winter Solstice, my family and I dip candles as a part of our celebration, and we remember that evening each time we light one throughout the year.

SUPPLIES

- ❋ Drop cloths or newsprint to cover your work area
- ❋ 5 pounds (2.3 kg) natural beeswax pellets
- ❋ Double boiler or slow cooker reserved solely for beeswax
- ❋ Candle making or candy thermometer (optional)
- ❋ Four 10-inch (25.5 cm) lengths candle wick (Braided or square braid cotton or linen in size #1 is ideal.)
- ❋ 8 metal washers or nuts of any size
- ❋ Utility knife or scissors

ACTIVE TIME: under 30 minutes

TOTAL TIME: under 2 hours

YIELD: 8 taper candles (3 to 4 inches, or 7.5 to 10 cm each)

INSTRUCTIONS

1. Cover your work area with heavy drop cloths or thick pads of newsprint. It's a good idea to cover the floor in your work area as well, choosing something that won't slip (like an old rug).

2. Fill your double boiler or slow cooker to the top with beeswax pellets (they will settle during heating). If using a double boiler, fill the bottom with water to the fill line (so the water does not touch the bottom of the melting pot) and then place the wax pot on top of the water. Place the double boiler over medium-high heat to melt. Alternatively, fill a slow cooker dedicated to wax with the pellets and place it on your covered countertop, plug in, and set it to high heat.

3. While your wax melts, prepare your wicks. Securely knot a washer or metal nut to each end of your wicks. These will help prevent the wicks from floating and encourage straighter candles.

4. As your wax melts, add additional pellets, if necessary, to bring the wax level to within 1 inch (2.5 cm) of the top of your pot.

5. When your wax is fully melted, check the temperature with your thermometer, if using. The ideal temperature for beeswax candles is around 165°F (74°C), within a few degrees.

6. Reduce the heat to low and prepare to prime your wicks. (Priming removes air bubbles and impregnates the wick with wax, ensuring a good burn when the candle is lit.) Pick up one wick and hold it at the center, with both washers hanging down to about an even length.

7. Carefully lower the wick into the wax, leaving 1 to 2 inches (2.5 to 5 cm) of wick above the wax level where you are holding it. If your wax pot is small, leave out as much of the extra wick as is needed to prevent the wicks from bending in the pot.

8. Hold the wicks in the wax until the bubbles stop rising, about 30 seconds.

9. Gently lift the wicks out of the wax and hold them above the wax pot to drip off and set. (Make sure your washers or wicks are not touching, which will cause your candles to fuse together.) If working as a group, each person takes a turn priming their wick as just described.

10. When all the wicks are primed, it's time to layer on your wax! Hold one pair of wicks, so the washers are not touching, and dip them more quickly into the wax than you did during priming. Each wick should remain in the wax for 2 to 4 seconds.

(continued)

NOTE

The directions that follow are for dipping short taper candles. Your candles will only be as tall as your wax is deep in your melting pot, so, depending on your pot, that can be quite petite! But, I think small candles are charming. If you want to make longer candles, you will need to purchase additional wax and a deep, narrow wax melting pot made specifically for candle dipping. (See the Resources section, page 137, for where to purchase.)

11. Lift and hold the wicks above the wax pot to let the candles drip and set. When drips are no longer forming, step aside from the wax pot with your pair of candles to let them fully cool, a minimum of 30 seconds. Check again that your washers or wicks are not touching; tease them apart if they are.

12. Repeat steps 10 and 11 (for all your candle pairs) four more times until there is a nice coating of wax covering your wick.

13. When your candle is cool enough to hold comfortably, use a utility knife or utility scissors to cut off the very bottom of your candle to remove the washer. Roll the candle between your hands to smooth out any rough spots caused by cutting.

14. Repeat steps 10 and 11 until your candle reaches your desired size. Let cool fully and then cut the wick to separate each pair of candles.

TROUBLESHOOTING

Following are some common problems that happen when learning to dip candles and how to fix them.

WAX IS NOT BUILDING UP ON THE CANDLE'S WICK WITH EACH DIP. Either your dipping time is too long (causing the wax to melt off the wick) or your wax is too hot. Try dipping the wick more quickly into the wax and let it cool thoroughly between each dip. If you don't see wax building up after four or five dips, the wax is too hot. Turn off the heat and let cool for 5 to 10 minutes before attempting to dip again. (Turn the heat back on if the wax begins to skin over on the top, indicating it has become too cool.)

CANDLES ARE LUMPY OR BUBBLY. The wax is too cold. Warm your wax to about 165°F (74°C), within a few degrees, if you are using a thermometer, or until the surface of your candles evens out during dipping. If desired, roll the warm candle gently between your hands to smooth out the lumps before continuing to dip. More dipping will even out most lumps and bumps, even without this added step.

CANDLES ARE CROOKED. You may be dipping your candle too deeply in your wax pot. Roll the still-warm candle between your palms to straighten it and then dip your candle straight up and down, without forcing it into the bottom of the pot.

If you've only just begun dipping, you may have removed your washer too soon, causing your wick to bend and float. Simply roll the candle between your hands while still warm (but not hot) after each dipping until the problem resolves.

NIGHT VISION FLASHLIGHT

You can modify your own regular flashlight with a piece of red plastic film using the instructions here to create a night vision flashlight. Red light does not negatively affect night vision, so a red flashlight is fine to use while your eyes adjust to the darkness, when you need a little extra help finding your way. Bring your Night Vision Flashlight along when you go Winter Stargazing (page 105) or set off on a Moonlit Night Walk (page 132).

SUPPLIES

* Scissors
* Transparent red cellophane or other red see-through material
* Flashlight or headlamp
* Rubber band

TIME: under 15 minutes

YIELD: 1 night vision flashlight

INSTRUCTIONS

1. Cut the red cellophane to about 1½ inches (3.8 cm) larger all around than the lens of your flashlight.

2. Wrap the cellophane over the flashlight head, securing it with your rubber band. Adjust as needed to prevent white light from leaking out around the edges.

SCENTED PLAY DOUGH

When I was a child, my mom often cooked up a batch of homemade play dough to keep my sister and me busy (and happy!) on cold, rainy days. We would spend hours at the kitchen table sculpting and playing. The recipe that follows is based on the one my mom used but updated with the addition of natural colorants.

INGREDIENTS

- ❋ ½ cup (120 ml) water
- ❋ ½ cup (63 g) white whole-wheat flour, plus more for kneading
- ❋ 2 tablespoons (36 g) table salt
- ❋ 1 tablespoon (9 g) cream of tartar
- ❋ 1 teaspoon olive oil or other liquid cooking oil
- ❋ 4 drops essential oil of your choice, try lavender, sweet orange, lemon, or lime (optional)

NATURAL COLORANTS (CHOOSE ONE PER BATCH)

- ❋ 1½ teaspoons dry hibiscus tea (for pink)
- ❋ 1¼ teaspoons matcha powder (for green)
- ❋ ½ teaspoon turmeric powder (for yellow)

TIME: under 20 minutes
YIELD: 3 ounces (85 g)

INSTRUCTIONS

1. In a small saucepan over high heat, bring the water to a boil. Add natural colorant as desired (if using). Cover the pan and steep for 20 minutes.

2. Meanwhile, in another saucepan, stir together the flour, salt, and cream of tartar to combine.

3. If using hibiscus tea as a colorant, strain out the tea leaves using a fine-mesh strainer set over a small bowl and compost or discard them. Add the tinted water and olive oil to your dry mixture and stir well to combine.

4. Place the pan over medium heat and cook the dough mixture, stirring constantly.

5. As your mixture cooks, it will begin as a wet, soupy consistency, then will become a thick paste. When the mixture begins to stick to the pan, reduce the heat to low and keep stirring. As the mixture thickens, it will eventually come together in a relatively smooth ball of dough with no remaining liquid. Total cooking time will be 2 to 5 minutes.

6. Remove from the heat and let your dough cool for 5 to 10 minutes or until cool enough to handle comfortably.

7. Lightly dust a work surface with flour and turn the dough out onto it. Knead until smooth.

8. If scenting your dough, make a dent in each dough ball using your index finger and add 4 drops of essential oil. Fold the dough around the essential oil and carefully knead and fold to work the scent throughout. Refrigerate your finished play dough in a tightly lidded container for up to 12 months. Let come to room temperature, as needed, for easier shaping.

TIP

Other natural dyes to experiment with include blue spirulina powder (blue), butterfly pea powder (purple), activated charcoal (grey), and instant coffee (brown). Begin with 1 teaspoon of each and adjust the quantity as desired to achieve the depth of color you want. Or, experiment with ingredients you have on hand to see what you might create!

HOMEMADE EGGNOG

Homemade eggnog is one of the tastiest winter treats I know. It's thick, warm, delicious . . . and it isn't difficult to make. Just milk, eggs, sweetener, and spices—plus some vigorous whisking!—and you're on your way to a mugful of cozy.

Is eggnog new to you? Think of it as ice cream's warm, drinkable cousin. It's the perfect treat on a cold winter night.

INGREDIENTS

* ❋ 4 cups (946 ml) full-fat dairy milk or nut milk
* ❋ ¼ cup (80 g) maple syrup, plus more to taste
* ❋ 2 eggs
* ❋ 3 egg yolks
* ❋ 1½ teaspoons vanilla extract
* ❋ 1½ teaspoons freshly grated nutmeg

TIME: under 20 minutes

YIELD: 4½ cups (about 1 L)

INSTRUCTIONS

1. In a medium-size pot over medium heat, stir together the milk, maple syrup, and nutmeg. Cook for 5 to 8 minutes until steaming hot, but below a boil.

2. While the milk warms, in a heatproof bowl or glass measuring cup, whisk the eggs and egg yolks to combine thoroughly. Set aside.

3. Find a partner to help you, so you can whisk and pour at the same time. When the milk is steaming hot, slowly drizzle 1 tablespoon (15 ml) of hot milk into the egg mixture while vigorously whisking the eggs to combine.

4. Repeat this process four to six more times until you've whisked at least ¼ cup (60 ml) of hot milk into the eggs. This process is called "tempering," and it keeps you from making scrambled eggs when you add them to the hot milk.

5. Drizzle the egg and milk mixture you just made into the remaining hot milk in your pot, whisking vigorously all the while.

6. When thoroughly combined, turn the heat under the pot to medium-low. Cook the eggnog for 2 to 5 minutes until it begins to bubble and thicken, whisking constantly.

7. Allow it to bubble gently for 1 to 2 minutes more and then remove from the heat. Let the eggnog cool for 5 minutes.

8. Stir in the vanilla.

9. Let cool until it reaches a still warm but drinkable temperature. If you like your eggnog silky smooth, you can use an immersion blender or a standard blender to purée it for about 30 seconds until smooth or pour the eggnog through a fine-mesh strainer to remove any lumps. (Never purée piping hot liquids in your blender, as they can explode out of the pitcher, causing serious burns.)

10. Serve in mugs, topped with a sprinkle of freshly grated nutmeg.

MAPLE LOLLIPOPS

In *Little House in the Big Woods*, Laura Ingalls Wilder recalls maple season at her grandparents' house in Wisconsin, where they slowly boiled down sap to make maple syrup to last them through the year. She also shares their tradition for making maple sugar candy by pouring the cooked-down syrup onto plates heaped with snow, transforming the hot liquid into soft candy in moments.

In this version, you can use snow, or if you live in a warmer climate, use a block of ice instead (see instructions that follow). Snow or ice—the results are equally delicious!

INGREDIENTS AND SUPPLIES

- ✳ Metal baking pan
- ✳ Clean snow or tray of ice
- ✳ 6 to 8 maple tree sticks or apple tree sticks (or use wooden skewers or ice pop sticks)
- ✳ ½ cup (160 g) pure maple syrup
- ✳ Cooking pot
- ✳ Candy thermometer (optional)

TIME: under 40 minutes

YIELD: 6 to 8 lollipops

INSTRUCTIONS

1. Fill a baking pan with clean snow, packing it down with your hands to create a somewhat solid snowpack in your pan. Place the tray of snow outside in the cold or inside in the freezer. If you live in a snow-free climate, begin by filling a metal baking pan of any size with 1 inch (2.5 cm) of water and then carefully transfer it to the freezer until solid. (If your freezer is too small to accommodate a baking pan, fill two or three plastic zip-top bags with water, seal, and lay flat in your freezer until frozen solid. Remove the bags and lay the slabs of ice in your baking tray before proceeding with the recipe.)

2. Arrange your sticks on the snow or ice, placing them about 2 inches (5 cm) apart. If you'd like more neat-looking lollies, make a depression in the snow overlapping ½ inch (1 cm) at the end of one stick, using a small, clean spice jar or other 1- to 2-inch (2.5 to 5 cm) round.

3. Return your tray to the freezer or cold outdoors.

4. With a grown-up helping, pour the maple syrup into a medium-size saucepan and place the pan over medium-high heat. Bring the syrup to a boil and then reduce the heat slightly to prevent boiling over. Stir constantly. If your syrup is especially frothy, add a drop of olive oil to reduce the chance of hot syrup boiling over.

5. Continue cooking your syrup until it reaches 240°F (115.5°C) on your candy thermometer (if using) or until it reaches the "soft ball" stage of candy making (see Tip).

6. Place your tray of snow or ice on a stable surface near your stove. Carefully transfer the hot syrup to a trivet near the tray and slowly pour the candy into 1-inch (2.5 cm) circles onto the snow, overlapping one end of each stick. Repeat until all the syrup has been poured.

7. Let cool completely, 2 to 3 minutes, before removing from the tray and enjoying your candy!

8. To store, blot melted snow or ice off the maple candy and transfer the lollipops to a waxed paper bag. The candy will soften if not consumed within a day but will still be tasty.

NOTE

This project is best done with at least one adult and one or more kids. While the maple syrup cooks and one person stirs, the others can arrange the sticks on the tray of snow or ice.

TIP

If you don't have a candy thermometer, you can still make maple candy! Fill a small saucepan with cold water and ice cubes. Every few minutes, place a drop of syrup into the icy water. If the syrup dissolves into the water, it isn't ready. If it forms a caramel-y droplet, you are almost there. The candy is ready when it forms a relatively hard drop of candy in the bottom of the pot. When you reach this stage, remove the syrup from the heat and proceed with the recipe.

ICE LANTERNS

Welcome guests to your winter home with a path lined with ice lanterns! They're perfect for your winter Celebration of Light or any dark evening when you want to create a little more beauty and magic outdoors.

SUPPLIES

* ❋ 1 medium to large empty plastic tub per lantern (from yogurt, ice cream, sour cream, etc.), washed and dried, if needed
* ❋ 1 small empty plastic tub per lantern, with a diameter at least 2 inches (5 cm) smaller than the medium tub it will be paired with (Small soup or tomato paste cans work well in a pinch!)
* ❋ Water
* ❋ Rubber bands or masking tape
* ❋ Tea light candles
* ❋ Matches

ACTIVE TIME: under 15 minutes

TOTAL TIME: 6 or more hours

INSTRUCTIONS

1. Fill your large tubs with 1 to 2 inches (2.5 to 5 cm) of water, filling each about one-fourth full.

2. If outdoor temperatures are below freezing, place the filled tubs out of direct sunlight on a level surface outside. If you live in a warmer climate, place them in the freezer, being careful to keep the tubs level. Freeze for 3 hours or more until solid.

3. Bring your tub indoors or remove them from the freezer. Nest a smaller tub inside each of the larger ones, securing them in the center with an X of rubber bands or masking tape holding them securely. (Don't worry if the smaller tub is at a bit of an angle due to the ice or a little off-center. Ice lanterns aren't meant to be perfect, and these little quirks are just part of their charm!)

4. Carefully fill the large tub to within ½ inch (1 cm) of the inner rim. If you overfill your outer tub and water pours into the inner one, empty it and begin again. Place the tubs outdoors again or in the freezer until solid, 3 or more hours or overnight.

5. Once the lanterns are thoroughly frozen, remove the tape or rubber bands. Fill the inner tubs with warm water to help release them from the ice. Remove the smaller tubs from the lanterns. Run warm water over the outside of the larger tubs until they also release. Your lanterns are done! Place them back outside in the cold (or in the freezer) until you are ready to use them.

6. At dusk, gather your ice lanterns, candles, and matches outside. Place a tea light candle inside each lantern and then arrange the lanterns along your path or porch. Avoid any overhanging tree branches or other fire hazards when you place your lanterns. Carefully light each ice lantern and then step back and enjoy the winter magic.

NOTE

The instructions here are for making one lantern at a time. My family has found it best to make them in batches, creating several lanterns at once. Repeat the process until you have the number of lanterns you want.

TIP

Although these lanterns were designed for outdoor use, they're beautiful inside as well. If you'd like to use your ice lanterns indoors, place them in a baking tray on a nonporous surface and remove melting ice, as needed, to prevent spills.

BUILD A SNOW FORT

Growing up in the wintery north, one of the highlights of the year for me was building a snow fort with my friends! My kids have grown up with this same tradition, and they relish every snow day, running outside to start work on a snow fort as soon as breakfast is done (sometimes sooner).

The snow forts that my family builds are based off a shelter called a quinzhee (the Athabaskan word for a traditional, native Canadian snow shelter). Quinzhees are created by piling snow into a mound, allowing it to settle and then hollowing out the inside. A well-built quinzhee is safe, solid, and surprisingly warm! Follow the instructions and you'll be cozied up inside your snow fort in no time.

SUPPLIES

* ❉ 1 foot (30 cm) or more of freshly fallen snow (Very wet snow is not suitable, but any other type will work.)
* ❉ 30 to 40 sticks each about the diameter of your finger and roughly 18 inches (45 cm) long
* ❉ Shovels
* ❉ Sled (optional)

ACTIVE TIME: under 2 hours

TOTAL TIME: 5 hours or more

YIELD: 1 impressive snow fort!

INSTRUCTIONS

1. Choose a site for your quinzhee that is away from fences, walls, trees, and other obstructions. Stomp out a circle in the snow, marking the outline of your quinzhee. A diameter of 6 to 8 feet (1.8 to 2.4 m) will suffice, allowing space for you and a friend, taking into account the 1-foot (30 cm)-thick walls.

2. Begin shoveling snow from outside your circle to the inside. Keep piling the snow until your snow mound is 4½ to 5 feet (1.4 to 1.5 m) high at the center.

SAFETY NOTES

When built properly, a quinzhee is safe and warm. But if you don't follow the instructions, your fort could collapse. Don't take chances! Follow the instructions as written.

(continued)

3. Allow your snow pile to settle for at least 3 hours. Through the settling process, the snow crystals lock together, forming a firm mass that will create a safe snow shelter.

4. Insert 1 stick straight into your quinzhee until 1 inch (2.5 cm) or less protrudes from the snow mound. Repeat this with the remaining sticks, inserting them about 1 foot (30 cm) apart all over the quinzhee. These sticks will help you estimate the thickness of your snow fort walls when you begin hollowing it out. When you expose the end of a stick with your shovel, you know the wall in that section is the proper thickness, and you can stop digging in that area.

5. Hollow out your quinzhee! Choose which side of your shelter you'll place the door. Typically, placing the door away from the wind is a great idea and will mean a cozier snow fort—but any side will do.

6. Using your shovel, begin scooping out a doorway that is big enough for you to fit through (about 2 feet, or 60 cm, across).

7. Now, it's time to hollow out your fort. Working from the doorway, continue digging into the show shelter. You will create a larger and larger opening, deeper, wider, and higher into your snow pile, creating the fort. It's useful to work with a friend during this process, with one person lying partially inside the shelter, pushing snow around their body to the outside, and another person pulling the snow away to discard it.

8. Keep digging! The first few minutes are the hardest, but once you see progress it's easy to keep at it. Take turns digging from the inside and moving snow from the outside. Before long, you'll be seated inside, removing snow from the walls and ceiling while sitting up. It's helpful at this stage to slide a sled through the doorway to fill with snow, making it easier to cart the snow away from the entrance.

9. When you've excavated down to the sticks throughout your snow fort, your quinzhee is done! Sit back and enjoy your hard work.

SAFETY NOTES

Follow these important guidelines and your quinzhee will be a safe, fun space to spend a winter day.

* Never climb on your quinzhee—before, during, or after piling the snow. Climbing on the fort weakens the structure and can cause it to collapse.

* After piling your snow, be certain to wait at least 3 hours before digging out your quinzhee. This creates a stable structure that you can safely hollow out. During this time the snow crystals lock together, increasing the strength of your structure. Digging out soon after piling up the snow creates weak walls that can fall.

* Work with a friend! Always have someone with you to help move snow away from the doorway. Especially at the beginning, it's a comfort to know a friend is just beyond the snow walls.

* In bitter cold temperatures, exposed skin can quickly become frostbitten. Keep skin covered and warm up inside as needed throughout the process.

MAPLE SNOW

Are you lucky enough to live in an area where the snow falls deep each winter? Fresh, deep, fluffy snow has a way of calling me outside to ski, hike, snowshoe, and play. It's my very favorite part of winter!

And transforming a bit of the clean, fluffy snow into a sweet winter treat? Well, I think that's simply a vital part of childhood in any snowy clime. If you don't live in a region with deep, clean snow, keep reading for a no-snow maple treat I dreamed up just for you!

INGREDIENTS AND SUPPLIES

* ❋ 4 small bowls, chilled
* ❋ 1 large bowl
* ❋ Large wooden or metal spoon
* ❋ Clean, freshly fallen snow
* ❋ ¼ cup (80 g) pure maple syrup

TIME: under 15 minutes for snow version; under 4 hours for no-snow variation

YIELD: 4 servings

INSTRUCTIONS

1. Place 4 soup or dessert bowls and a large wooden or metal spoon outside to chill. (Unbreakable bowls are best, as you'll be carrying them around outside in a few minutes while you gather your snow.) Let the bowls chill for 5 minutes or so and then bundle up in your outdoor gear.

2. Using your large bowl and spoon, fill the bowl with clean, fluffy snow from the very top of your snowbank, porch, or yard. Scoop only freshly fallen snow, not the harder layers below. Gather snow only from areas where birds, pets, and wildlife have not recently traveled. When your serving bowl is full, head back to the kitchen!

3. Bring your chilled smaller bowls inside now.

4. Look over your large bowl of snow. Scoop out and discard any snow that contains bits of tree bark or other debris. (We want only the cleanest snow for eating!)

5. Fill each small bowl with about 1½ cups (355 ml) of fresh snow.

6. Drizzle the snow in each bowl with 1 tablespoon (20 g) of maple syrup and enjoy.

NO-SNOW VARIATION

Not everyone lives in a snowy place! With that in mind, here's your ticket to maple snow, even if your winters are warm.

INGREDIENTS

* 2 cups (475 ml) water
* 1 cup (320 g) pure maple syrup

INSTRUCTIONS

1. In a medium-size bowl, stir together the water and maple syrup until well combined.

2. Transfer the bowl to a wide, flat-bottomed storage container, seal the container, and place it in the freezer.

3. Freeze for 6 to 8 hours, stirring after the first hour, and then stirring again every 30 to 45 minutes, scraping the ice crystals away from the sides and bottom of your container.

4. Continue stirring and freezing until it reaches the consistency of an icy sorbet.

5. Serve in chilled bowls.

FOLDED WINDOW STARS

Winter often means more time spent indoors. And, in many regions, it can mean a dreary view out the front window. Lacking the vibrant greens of summer, gray winter can get us down. So, why not brighten up that winter view with colorful, folded window stars? When made of translucent paper, they all but glow in the afternoon light. It's my favorite way to bring a little cheer to any gray view.

Window stars are traditionally made with a translucent paper sold as "kite paper" (see the Resources section, page 137, for where to buy). They're also lovely when folded with any other thin, colorful paper you have on hand. Even recycled office paper will work!

SUPPLIES

* ✳ Kite paper or other lightweight paper (ideally translucent, but use what you have)
* ✳ Ruler (optional, if your paper is not precut into squares)
* ✳ Scissors (if your paper is not precut into squares)
* ✳ Glue stick

TIME: under 15 minutes per star

TIME: 1 window star

INSTRUCTIONS

1. If your paper did not arrive as precut squares, use your ruler and scissors to measure and cut squares from your paper. Window stars can be made from paper squares of any size, but I find 6- and 8-inch (15 and 20 cm) squares are most manageable.

2. Cut a total of 8 squares in the color or colors of your choice.

3. Begin folding your squares. Choose one piece of kite paper and fold neatly in half along the diagonal. Use your fingernail or the side of your ruler to create a nice, crisp fold.

4. Open the paper and bring one edge (corner) of the paper to your diagonal fold line. Align this paper edge with the fold and crease it firmly.

5. Repeat with the adjoining edge (corner) on the opposite side of the crease, forming a kite shape.

6. Without opening your two newest folds, bring each "kite" side in to the center line and crease again, creating a thinner, narrower kite.

7. Repeat with 7 more pieces of paper.

8. Carefully apply a small dab of glue to the inside of each of your folded flaps to secure them.

9. Assemble your window star. Place 1 folded square on the table in front of you with your folded sides up and the narrow point aiming away from you (toward 12:00).

10. Place a small dab of glue at the base, below the folded edges, and on the right side of the center crease only.

11. Take a second folded square and overlap the base with the first piece, aligning the bottom left edge with the midline of the first piece, the long point aimed toward about 2:00.

12. Apply a dab of glue to the bottom right of the second square and then lay a third piece on top, aligning again with the centerline of the previous piece.

13. Repeat until 7 of your 8 folded papers are connected, creating a neat starburst pattern.

14. To place the final piece, apply glue to the bottom right corner of the last piece you placed, as well as the bottom right of the remaining folded paper square.

15. Place as previously, but tuck the final piece under the first one and press to secure. Your window star is complete! Hang it in a sunny place to display using a dab of glue or a small piece of clear tape.

DRIED CITRUS GARLAND

Sometimes, we need a little warm, sunshine-y cheer to brighten a cold winter's night. Enter Dried Citrus Garland! Made with supplies that are easy to find, they're a snap to make and will keep your house feeling cozy all winter long.

SUPPLIES

* ❋ 8 to 10 oranges, ruby grapefruit, or a combination
* ❋ Sharp kitchen knife
* ❋ Cutting board
* ❋ Cotton towel
* ❋ Food dehydrator or oven
* ❋ Baking sheets fitted with metal cooling racks (optional, if using the oven)
* ❋ Baker's twine, cotton string, or embroidery floss
* ❋ Sewing needle to fit your twine

ACTIVE TIME: under 45 minutes

TOTAL TIME: 12 to 24 hours

YIELD: two 6-foot (1.8 m) garlands

INSTRUCTIONS

1. Slice your unpeeled citrus fruits into ⅛- to ¼-inch (3 to 6 mm) rounds. Blot on both sides to absorb excess moisture, using a cotton cloth or paper towels.

2. If using a dehydrator, arrange your citrus slices on your dehydrator trays. If using the oven, arrange the slices on the cooling racks placed on baking sheets. If you don't have cooling racks, blot the slices well and place them directly on your baking sheets.

3. Dehydrate the citrus slices according to your dehydrator's instructions for 8 to 12 hours. If using the oven, set it to 200°F (93°C) and place the baking sheets in the oven. Open the oven door every now and then to release humidity. If you are not using cooling racks, flip your citrus slices every 2 hours or so to ensure proper drying.

4. Continue dehydrating until the slices feel crisp and fully dry, 8 to 12 hours, depending on your drying method and house humidity. The actual drying time will vary, depending on the size and thickness of your citrus slices. Feel them to test for dryness, and when they are crisp (though slightly tacky to the touch), your slices are ready. Remove them from the oven or dehydrator.

5. Cut a 6-foot (1.8 m) length of twine and thread it onto your needle.

6. Thread one citrus slice onto the needle, pushing the needle through the flesh close to the peel. Slide the threaded citrus slice to about 1 foot (30 cm) from the far end of your string and securely knot it in place. Push your needle back through the citrus fruit, close to the peel and 1 to 2 citrus sections from where you first pushed the needle through. This will create a line of twine across your fruit, allowing them to face you when displayed.

7. String another citrus slice onto your needle, repeating the same threading pattern.

8. Repeat this process until you have roughly 4 feet (1.2 m) of citrus slices strung together or you run out of fruit!

9. When you have strung your last slice, repeat the knotting process you did at the beginning to secure the last slice. Trim your tails to be roughly even, about 1 foot (30 cm) each.

NOTE

If your house is humid, your citrus slices with soften with time. Pop them back in the oven or dehydrator, if needed, to keep them dry and crisp.

When thoroughly dry, store in an airtight container for use year after year. Citrus slices will keep indefinitely if stored dry. Discard the garland if mold develops on the fruit.

MIX IT UP!

Instead of using only oranges and grapefruit, experiment with a variety of citrus fruits. Add blood oranges and lemons, or experiment with limes, clementines, even kumquats!

Or, mix in other non-citrus elements to your garland like fresh cranberries, pinecones, or fresh rosemary sprigs. In all but the most humid climates, the fresh berries and rosemary will dry while the garland is on display.

For younger children, citrus slices can be strung sideways, threading the slices through the hole in the center with a blunt needle. The slices will stack together, but with a little patience (or adult assistance), they can be separated for display.

My family's Winter Solstice celebration is my favorite holiday of the year. Small, intimate, and cozy, it's the perfect way to set intentions for a lovely year to come.

Create your own simple traditions to celebrate the longest night.

Enjoy any or all of the winter festivities following or create your own celebration with recipes and projects found in this chapter.

HOLIDAY: Winter Solstice

LOCATION: Celebrate the longest night in your favorite, cozy nest. If you can arrange for snuggly blankets, twinkle lights, or a crackling fire, all the better.

DECORATIONS: Dried Citrus Garland (page 128), Folded Window Stars (page 126), Ice Lanterns (page 118), and homemade Beeswax Candles (page 108)

FOOD AND DRINK: A pot of soup or chili, Homemade Eggnog (page 114), and your family's favorite holiday cookies

ACTIVITIES AND PARTY FAVORS: Make Pinecone Bird Feeders (page 106), jot down your Wishes for The Coming Year (page 136), and enjoy a peaceful Moonlit Night Walk (page 132). If you have a suitable location for a fire, enjoy a Winter Bonfire (page 134) and then send your guests home with jars of a homemade tea blend or a handmade candle (page 108).

MOONLIT NIGHT WALK

We so rarely set off into the night without a flashlight or headlamp lighting our way. But when we do, a whole new world reveals itself. We move slowly and mindfully, aware of each stone underfoot and sounds from the treetops. It's a magical way to explore the night!

SUPPLIES

* Backpack with a basic first-aid kit, Night Vision Flashlight (page 111) or headlamp, and filled water bottle
* One or more family member or friends to accompany you on your journey
* Familiar hiking path
* Supportive winter boots, hiking boots, or other footwear with good traction
* Appropriate clothing for the weather where you live
* Wristwatch with a timer (optional)
* Snowshoes, if snow is deep in your region (optional)

TIME: 30 minutes to 1 hour

INSTRUCTIONS

1. Check your backpack and night walk supplies to be sure you have everything.

2. Tell a friend or family member where you are hiking and what time you expect to return. Let them know you will call them when you're back inside.

3. Head to your hiking trail. Check the time when you arrive so you know how long you have walked before you turn back.

4. If you used a flashlight to get there, turn it off now and spend a few moments with your light switched off, allowing your eyes to adjust to the darkness.

5. Slip your headlamp or flashlight into your pack to reduce the temptation to switch it on!

6. Set off slowly down your hiking trail, moving your feet mindfully in the darkness. Step as softly as you can and talk in hushed voices so as not to overpower the stillness and quiet of the night.

7. How much you can see will vary greatly depending on how bright the moon is and whether there are any street lights or buildings nearby that are adding light to your environment. As your eyes continue to adjust to the darkness, you'll become aware of more and more details before you. Pay attention to how different this familiar path feels by moonlight than it does by day.

8. Walk your path for 10 to 15 minutes before turning back and heading toward home. If desired, set a timer on your watch to alert you when it's time to turn back and then turn it off without illuminating the watch face. (Even the small amount of light from a watch or phone can affect your night vision, making it much more difficult to see.)

9. On the return trip, pay attention to how much easier it is to see details around you because of the time your eyes have had to adjust to the darkness.

10. When you arrive home, let your friend or family member know you are back!

RODS AND CONES

Your eyes include two different types of receptors: one set for low-light vision, the other for bright-light vision. The bright-light receptors, called cones, allow you to perceive color in your surroundings, while the low-light receptors, called rods, do not. This is why when you allow your eyes to adjust to the darkness, the world looks black, white, and gray.

A WINTER BONFIRE

The Winter Solstice is a celebration of the returning of the light. This longest night and shortest day of the year mean that, beginning the very next morning, the days will grow longer and, in time, spring will return. What better way to celebrate the light than to create one of your own? A winter bonfire is a spirited way to celebrate the longest, darkest night.

SUPPLIES

* Campfire circle or pit
* Larger, dry firewood
* Newspaper (black-and-white sheets only), or shredded birch bark
* Small, dry twigs or other kindling
* Matches

TIME: 45 minutes or more

INSTRUCTIONS

1. Prepare your fire pit. Remove any snow, dry grass, sticks, or other debris from the inside of your fire circle or pit. Repeat this process on the outside of your fire pit, clearing away a minimum of 2 feet (60 cm) around the ring.

2. If your fire pit is wet, place a layer of dry firewood on the ground inside your fire ring to provide a dry place on which to light your fire.

3. Begin by placing a handful of loosely crumpled newspaper or shredded birch bark in the center of your fire area. Place two thumb-size sticks on opposite sides of your newspaper. Then, place two more perpendicular to these, creating a square of sticks around your paper. This method of fire making is called the "log cabin" style because sticks are placed in a similar fashion to how logs are laid when building a cabin.

4. Repeat this stick placement until you have a few layers and your "cabin" is about 6 inches (15 cm) tall.

5. Inside your "cabin," place a few of your smallest twigs. Prop them against one side of the stacked sticks at an angle, so they lean across and above the newspaper.

6. Repeat this process with more sticks until you have a good amount of tinder to catch when you light the newspaper. Continue layering sticks, adding gradually larger twigs until you have added a few good handfuls.

7. Before you light the fire, make sure you have more dry kindling to feed the fire, as well as a few small pieces of dry firewood about the diameter of your wrist.

8. Carefully strike a match and slip it in through a slat in your "cabin" toward the ground. Light your newspaper in several places. Your newspaper should begin to burn and will light the smallest twigs first, which will ignite the larger twigs.

9. As your kindling begins to burn, slowly add more kindling or small pieces of firewood to keep the fire burning. Eventually, your "cabin" will begin to burn, and you can lean larger pieces of wood against it, feeding your winter bonfire.

NOTE

See Campfire Safety (page 97) for an important safety review around building fires.

WISHES FOR THE COMING YEAR

As one year draws to a close, a brand-new year begins. It's a wonderful feeling to look ahead, to a clean, fresh beginning. Set your dreams and wishes for the coming year by jotting them onto birch bark or paper and then tossing them into the fire. As the bundles burn, I love to think of the intentions written there drifting up with the wisps of smoke, to take shape in the coming months.

SUPPLIES

- ✳ 2 or 3 pieces of birch bark or watercolor paper for each participant
- ✳ Pencils
- ✳ Kitchen string, twine, or paper ribbon
- ✳ Scissors

TIME: under 30 minutes

INSTRUCTIONS

1. Place birch bark in a basket or bowl in the center of a table. Arrange the pencils around the basket and place twine and scissors on the table within reach.

2. Instruct your guests to write down their wishes, dreams, or aspirations for the coming year on a strip of bark and then roll it up and tie it with a piece of string. These small scrolls can be placed in their pockets until the fire is ready.

3. When the fire is burning, you and your guests can take out your bundles as you feel ready and gently toss them into the fire.

VARIATION

For pre-writers, set out colored pencils and larger sheets of paper or bark. Younger children can illustrate their wishes, instead of writing them down.

RESOURCES

ACORN CAPS: If you can't find any locally, purchase online at www.etsy.com.

BEESWAX: If you can't find beeswax locally, shop online at www.bulkapothecary.com.

BINOCULARS FOR STARGAZING: If you already own binoculars for birdwatching, try them for stargazing as well! Or look into purchasing a pair that can do both (the Oberwerk 8×42 ED come highly recommended).

CHENILLE STICKS: High quality pipe cleaners made with biodegradable cotton are available at www.achildsdream.com.

DRIED HERBS: If you can't source herbs locally, purchase high quality, organic herbs at www.mountainroseherbs.com.

PLANTING TREES: Find ways to get involved in community tree planting by inquiring at your local township, city, or regional government, or search online at www.arborday.org.

TAPER CANDLE DIPPING VAT: You can purchase one online at www.betterbee.com.

TERRARIUM MOSS: Seek out sustainably harvested or cultivated moss locally or try online at www.mossacres.com.

WOODEN PEG DOLLS: Check your local craft supply shop or buy online at www.caseyswood.com.

WOOL FELT, WOOL ROVING, AND KITE PAPER: All can be purchased at Paper Scissors Stone, www.waldorfsupplies.com. This local-to-me online shop specializes in high quality children's art and school supplies.

RECOMMENDED READING

Following are some of my favorite books to encourage outdoor exploration and unplugged fun.

Home Grown by Ben Hewitt

I Love Dirt! 52 Activities to Help You and Your Kids Discover the Wonders of Nature by Jennifer Ward

Last Child in the Woods by Richard Louv

Outdoor Science Lab for Kids by Liz Lee Heinecke

Play the Forest School Way by Jane Worroll and Peter Houghton

Simplicity Parenting by Kim John Payne

"Stargazing: Explore Celestial Mythology" in *A Child's Introduction to the Night Sky* by Michael Driscoll

Vitamin N: The Essential Guide to a Nature-Rich Life by Richard Louv

GRATITUDE

Though it's my name printed on the cover, I did not write this book alone. Dozens of friends, old and new, helped along the way. The list following includes only some of my many helpers but is incomplete at best. If you offered a hand, an idea, or your energy and don't see your name here, do write it in with a sparkly pen, won't you? You deserve my heartfelt thanks and I regret missing you when I jotted my list.

To Pete, thank you once again for juggling all of the things in our life to make space for me to write, play, and make countless messes while writing this book. You are forever my greatest cheerleader, and I can't imagine life any other way. (I promise to clean up all of the acorn caps, bubble wands, and teacups that are scattered about the house soon-ish.)

To my kids, thank you for your childhood-long enthusiasm for all things unplugged, crafty, and adventurous. You have inspired me from the start and taught me how to be a better human.

Sage, thank you for being my first and finest teacher. You inspired many of these projects in your younger days. I'm glad you managed to endure a few photographs for these pages, when I sullied our otherwise peaceful adventures with the click of my shutter.

Lupine, I am grateful for your heroic fingernail scrubbing and unflagging enthusiasm as you dove in and helped out with nearly every project we undertook for this book. Your squeals of, "Oh, Mama! This sounds so fun! Can we do it right now?" coaxed me through many long writing days and helped me see the magic on every page. How grateful I am every day for the joy and enthusiasm you share wherever you go.

A heaping dose of gratitude goes to my "councy" friend, Genie, for a garden's worth of marigolds (also cucumbers and green beans) and her keen proofreading eye. You are an unflaggingly fine and generous friend. Thank you as well to my friend and illustrator Lucky Nielson, whose captivating artwork can be see on page 18. And gratitude to Jackie Currie of Happy Hooligans for sharing her bubble juice recipe (page 69).

And to the many new and old friends who jumped in so willingly and playfully to assist with photographs, you were marvelous! What would I have done without you? Local friends Alyson, Griffin, Magnolia, Amara, Addisu, Lena, Zuri, Wynne, Ruby, Henry, Sophia, Helena, Soloman, Roman, Michelle, and Chris; my lifelong dear one Ami, along with Usha, Ashok, Ettan, and Luke; the phenomenal crew at the Milwaukee Coalition for Children's Mental Health: Kamaria, Azariah, Genesis, Dehemi'ah, Ida, Bheyon, Brushon, Burron, Amy, Jeremiah, Matilda, Aniela, William, Jocelyn, Michael, Madeline, Leah, Blake, Steve, and Umair; and my dear Icelandic pal, Leo; thank you from my heart.

And finally, to my blog readers and followers. Thank you for encouraging me year after year to write about the simple joys of our simple life. Thank you for pushing me to share more about my parenting journey and asking me to write a book for families. Here it is.

ABOUT THE AUTHOR

Rachel Jepson Wolf lives with her husband and two kids, Lupine and Sage, on a scruffy homestead in rural Wisconsin. Her days are spent writing, foraging, crafting, homeschooling, and running LüSa Organics, her sustainable body care company.

Rachel is happiest when hanging out with her family, exploring the forest, in the company of a dog, knitting, drinking tea, or sitting beside a crackling campfire (or better yet, all of the above).

You can find Rachel online, where she blogs about parenting, homeschooling, and unplugged imperfection at lusaorganics.typepad.com, or explore her herbal body care products at www.rachelwolfclean.com. Her first book, *Herbal Adventures*, is also a whole lot of fun.

INDEX